# Finance Is Personal

# Finance Is Personal

## MAKING YOUR MONEY WORK FOR YOU IN COLLEGE AND BEYOND

Kim Stephenson and Ann B. Hutchins

*Foreword by Steven G. Blum*

 PRAEGER™

An Imprint of ABC-CLIO, LLC
Santa Barbara, California • Denver, Colorado

Copyright © 2015 by Kim Stephenson and Ann B. Hutchins

**Library of Congress Cataloging-in-Publication Data**

Stephenson, Kim.
   Finance is personal: making your money work for you in college and beyond/Kim Stephenson and Ann B. Hutchins; foreword by Steven G. Blum.
      pages cm
   Includes bibliographical references and index.
   ISBN 978–1–4408–3436–3 (hard copy: alk. paper) — ISBN 978–1–4408–3437–0 (ebook) 1. College students—Finance, Personal. 2. Budgets, Personal. I. Hutchins, Ann B. II. Title.
HG179.S83467   2015
332.024—dc23            2015009780

ISBN: 978–1–4408–3436–3
EISBN: 978–1–4408–3437–0

19  18  17  16  15      1  2  3  4  5

This book is also available on the World Wide Web as an eBook.
Visit www.abc-clio.com for details.

Praeger
An Imprint of ABC-CLIO, LLC

ABC-CLIO, LLC
130 Cremona Drive, P.O. Box 1911
Santa Barbara, California 93116-1911

This book is printed on acid-free paper ∞

Manufactured in the United States of America

# Contents

# Foreword

My book and my courses all start with a question. Indeed, it is my favorite question in the world, "What is a good outcome?" *Finance Is Personal* also starts with a question and it is in the same spirit. Prior to figuring out the *how*, it is critically important to examine the *why*.

In that respect, Kim Stephenson and Ann Hutchins have produced a book on personal finance that stands apart from others. *Finance Is Personal* focuses on good outcomes for each particular person, as distinct from what is a "financial win" in technical terms that may actually be less than optimal regarding the individual's health, happiness, or well-being.

It is exceptional in another respect. I've written, lectured, and consulted on the difficulties of getting good advice about personal finance. Among the problems is a pervasive imbalance of information. When one party to a transaction knows a great deal more about the subject than the other, there is the potential for exploitation. Most financial practitioners have command of a great many industry practices and norms that are far beyond the knowledge of even very smart "regular people." They also have experience and training in various routines, techniques, and tricks-of-the-trade that give them an enormous advantage over their clients. An economist would describe this as an "asymmetry of information" between the advisor and the client.

Even the advisor who endeavors to be a "true professional" (and uses greater knowledge *solely* to advance the client's interests) is lacking something essential. The expert is without sufficient information about the client. It is only the client who knows those needs, desires, and preferences that will be necessary to craft a specifically "good outcome." Here the book opens the most important of doors. Using findings from psychology, neuroscience, and behavioral finance, the authors show how readers can use their unique and extensive knowledge of themselves to determine a range of best possible outcomes in the light of their individual circumstances. Only the individual possesses all the necessary information. Using the insights and exercises in the book, the reader comes to a greater perception of his or her own goals, needs, and desires. Once in possession of this self-understanding, she or he can negotiate the process of financial planning from a position of relative strength.

Many people believe they are effective pursuing their very best outcome already. Some of them are mistaken. They face two significant obstacles. The first is that a focus on external matters of finance will leave them vulnerable to be taken advantage of. As the authors point out, they would be better advised to concentrate first on the particulars of their own situation. After all, who knows more about you than you do?

The second stumbling block is the danger of becoming distracted. Financial education, as typically offered, tends to emphasize technical information. It is sometimes obsessed with particular financial instruments and the mathematics surrounding them. The focus is on what types of investments are available, probabilities of future events, ways to insure against financial calamities, and so on. These nuts and bolts are not sufficiently correlated with where one is trying to go. Indeed, they can easily become a distraction that obscures the more important exploration. What is the individual really trying to achieve? I frequently encounter people who have been encouraged to focus on the minutia of finance rather than the fundamental questions of how best to achieve the good outcomes they desire for themselves.

This book also stands out for the way it addresses the overarching problem of honesty in financial services. This is, of course, a critical question in light of the stakes. The world of finance is both complicated and intimidating, yet it is crucial to so much that we all hold dear. Our comfort, success, retirement, health, and happiness hang in the balance. A significant error can reverberate for a lifetime. It is imperative that we do one of two things: learn for ourselves or find guides who are highly knowledgeable, honest, and trustworthy.

Despite their claims, though, not everyone who makes a living offering financial advice is sufficiently knowledgeable and honest. So the great problem is finding professionals who are worthy of our trust. *Finance Is*

*Personal* is distinctive for asserting that the search begins with the clients themselves. The authors suggest that the reader is the central figure in any search for trustworthy advice. Their book offers tools for becoming the readers' own best guide through the complexities of financial decision making. With singular insight into their own values, desires, and ambitions, they are the truest expert on the proper direction of their financial life. With the proper guidance and training, they will be best equipped to seek out any external guidance needed. The argument, in essence, is that the individual can trust himself or herself. That is the necessary place to start the inquiry.

Anyone can benefit from reading *Finance Is Personal*. Regardless of age or degree of financial sophistication, something of value is offered to the reader. While the book puts particular emphasis on students, any seeker of knowledge can benefit from the insights, exercises, and wisdom the authors are offering within these pages. Here is an opportunity to build a sound basis upon which to negotiate your way to continuing good outcomes in your financial life.

**Steven G. Blum teaches in the Department of Legal Studies and Business Ethics at the Wharton School of Business and is the author of *Negotiating Your Investments: Use Proven Negotiation Methods to Enrich Your Financial Life***

# Preface

This is a book about how you can handle your money in order to get the life you want. When we were mapping it out we aimed to make it really helpful—the kind of book you'd keep referring to and your parents would say "I wish I'd read that when I was going to college."

When we actually set out to write it, we agreed on many things, but four were key:

First, that you are being asked to make more decisions about your money, earlier in life, than any previous generation. Second, that much of the information about "money and you" is telling you what you *should* and *must not* do with your money, when you are old enough to make those decisions and figure out how you want your money to work for you if you have good information. Third, that it should be written as if we were having a conversation, because it's easier to have conversations about money in the same way you have conversations about sports, music, or what's for dinner—why should discussing money be some weird ritual? And fourth, that it should be a conversation that wasn't exclusive to one gender or ethnicity (or any other group) and didn't assume you were an expert, or even interested, in finance.

So we took the most useful research, based on ideas that really work in life (not just in theory): Research that speaks to an audience going to college today and allows you to make your own decisions about your own money without telling you what you should do.

We'd both worked (and become qualified) in finance and also in coaching, psychology, and other *people* areas, so we knew that *you* are really complicated and are far more difficult to understand than money. So we worked on helping you to understand your own thinking, why you feel the way you do, and how you can think and feel differently if that's going to help you. You can learn the facts about money if you need them, but those facts are not nearly as important or complex as you are.

And we worked on speaking to a diverse college-going population that has a lot more financial responsibility than any previous generation.

In short, we set out to write a book that would turn around the conventions of telling you what to do, ignoring your personality and bombarding you with facts about money. We wanted the book to be a conversation about you, about how complex and important you are, and about how you can use money to have the life you want, whoever you are.

To make it useful and research based, we relied on our combined training and learning over the years, and to make it practical, we base suggestions and exercises on things we know work because we use them. And because this is about you, we decided that instead of "Ann discovered this ... " or "Kim uses this method with clients ... " which sounds clumsy, awkward, and beside the point, we'd write everything to *you*, the reader, as if we (either one of us!) were sitting with you. And we'd talk as "I" whether the "I" was Kim or Ann. The book is a joint effort, and as we wrote it, we discussed the contents to make sure we were giving you good information and useful tools in the clearest possible way. *Who* brought up the idea in the first place was irrelevant (and we forgot anyhow). This has been a collaboration in all the best senses. So that means you can imagine whoever you want to work with you. The book is a discussion between you and me, and I really hope that you will enjoy it, find it useful, quote it to people, and suggest your parents read it!

Chapter 1

# Going to College

You're off to college (or maybe you're there already). Why?

That might seem a strange question for a book about personal finance. But it's the most important question if you want to manage your money well.

In case you don't see why it's important, or why I'm asking, let me explain a few things:

1. I've written the book as if we were having a coaching session, because I've found that works.
2. I break off regularly to explain things that people usually ask me to explain. If you find the point obvious, great; you're clearly much smarter than most people I see!
3. I ask a lot of questions, which might require some thinking so you may need to go away and consider the question and come back to the book later.

If you don't see why the reason you are going to college is so important, it's point 1 (what I'd do in a coaching session) and an example of point 3 (a question to think about).

And here's point 2 (the break to explain what people usually ask me to explain):

*Motives drive the world—"why" is a much stronger question than "what" or "how."*

If you really, really want something, you're more likely to put in the effort to get it than if you would quite like it but it doesn't really matter. If you want it, you have a really strong "why should I do this." On the other hand, if you don't really care about it at all, you've got very little motivation to overcome any obstacles, so you're likely to give up as soon as the going gets tough, because why would you work hard to achieve something you don't care about?

Think about why you are going to college. Is it to be able to follow a career you really want, to establish your independence, to have a fantastic social life, because your parents want you to, because you don't know what else to do?

Whatever your answer, write it down, because that answer is the key to what you want your money to do for you.

If you know that you really, really want that college experience, the education, or whatever it is you're after, you'll study hard, you'll work at managing your money so you can get the most out of the experience, you'll change your behavior to give you the best chance to achieve what you want. If you don't care—well, what do you think will happen when you don't like a particular course or a professor, your money is running out, or you're getting criticized for your lifestyle?

Which leads me to several more important points:

4. You are way more important than your money—there's plenty of money; there's only one of you.

5. Your future is important. The money is just one way for you to get where you want, how you want and with what you want; it's just a tool.

6. The book is therefore more about you and your thinking than about money.

7. If you're smart enough to go to college, you're smart enough to focus on the important bit, *you,* and get that right before you worry about the trivial bit, *the money.*

8. You're also smart enough to look up facts on the Internet and don't need this book to give you facts like tax rates, Federal Student Aid budgets, and so on that change every year and will go out of date before the book is even published.

9. And you're smart enough to apply general learning to your own situation and extract principles from stories.

10. You're also a human being, so you like stories!

So the way I've arranged most of the book is to give true stories or composites of true stories (with the names and some details changed) that illustrate points. I've asked some questions that you can think about and ask yourself to help you apply the key issues to your own case. And I've tried to anticipate questions, not about stuff that you can look up for yourself, but about the ways you might think about finding solutions for yourself and judging which of the millions of pieces of information out there (on the Internet, and elsewhere) are actually useful to you.

And now here's a story—based on a composite of some real clients.

Meet Terri. She's 18. She's got a good relationship with her parents; they want to help her through college (neither of them were able to go), but they don't have much money to help her. When I ask her "why are you going to college," she says that she wants to be an architect. She wants to design buildings that are practical, but beautiful and that give the people living in them a real lift. She's unbelievably excited. I don't have to work with her to find out what colleges offer the courses she needs to qualify, what the subsequent training needed is, what the fees are, and so on (although if I did, I could find the information in less than half an hour without moving from my desk). She knows all that. And if you really want to do something as much as she wants to study and do architecture, if you have as strong a "why" for going where you're going and doing what you're doing, you'll know it all too.

What I need to ask her is "what's her plan for qualifying?" Is she going to go straight on to a graduate degree; will she study all the time, not have a social life and save her money for books? She knows her own character and I don't (not yet, anyway), so I want to find out whether she has got realistic ideas about what is possible. And I want to know whether she's got any ideas about how she's going to fund studies: will she work part time (and if so, at what), has she got prospects for a summer job or a job between degree and postgraduate study—maybe in an architect's office? Has she established some contacts that she can ask about opportunities for work, internships, advice, help with student projects? Does she know where she's going to live (on campus, at home, in rented accommodation off campus), and what she's going to eat (live on burgers, have every meal in the canteen, pool resources with her friends and take turns cooking)?

When I know what detail she's gone into about practical issues, we've got a firm base. She's got the most important part, the motivation. She's also got a basic plan for getting to the position she really wants to be in, a working architect. College is just a step on the way. But what is she going to do about money?

If she does want to take up all the opportunities, the trips to visit buildings around the country (or abroad), the visits to leading firms' offices, and so on, she has to have the money to do it. If she wants to do the optional reading, maybe she needs the money for that or at least to know what she needs so she can start working with the librarians and other *gatekeepers* to allow her access to the interesting Journals, the out of print books, and so on without having to pay for them.

And although she might have a social life based around her high-school friends and her new architect-based lifestyle, she's probably going to want at least a bit of money to socialize with her classmates—or it's going to be a pretty lonely four or five years for much of the time.

Which is all in addition to the costs of rent, food, tuition, and so on.

Notice, there is no magic solution. But what Terri has now is the beginning of a practical plan. She's got the motivation to get her over the obstacles, to drive her to find ways to create income and contacts (like summer jobs in an architect's office), to find economical resources (like making contact with the library staff), to find a good balance between her social life now and her plans for the future, and to have a decent balanced diet without having to work 24/7 to pay for it.

Now meet Brad. He's in a similar position to Terri, with parents he's close to who are keen for him to get to college and have the chances they didn't have themselves, but who don't have much money to spare.

The financial advice that Terri and Brad would get from most people is the same, because they're in the same situation financially. But they are worlds apart in identifying their "why," and that's the key issue.

When I ask Brad "why are you going to college," he says because his parents want him to go. He doesn't really know what he wants to do with his life. College sounds like a good idea because he's been brought up to believe that college means success, but he doesn't really know what job he wants or what he wants to study. His father is very keen for him to become a CPA—because it's secure, it gives a good income and Brad got good grades for math all through high school. His mother doesn't mind what he does but would like him to become a professional.

When I ask Brad about what colleges run courses that would suit him, he doesn't know. He's opted for one that seems convenient, that some friends are going to. He doesn't have a plan for qualifying, because the idea isn't his, it's his parents'.

We can try to plan his finances, but how are we going to do that? How do we plan for work experience, for extra reading in areas that he's particularly interested in, and so on, when his plan is not really his at all? How do we work out a balance between funding for the future and funding his immediate needs, when he doesn't really know what he wants?

That's why I ask "why are you going to college"—because the reason you're going is the key to how you start planning your money.

If you aren't sure, if you're more like Brad than Terri, let's take a step back from college for a moment.

Would you like to live a happy life?

Dumb question, right? Who doesn't want to be happy? But if you want it, wouldn't it be a good idea to have a look at what makes people in general, and you in particular, happy?

There are lots of assumptions about this. People think that having lots of money makes you happy. Having material possessions, vacation homes, cars, a yacht, is a guarantee of happiness, right?

Well, think of it this way; if wealth and possessions made you happy, nobody rich would ever commit suicide—but they do. If money was the most important factor, then studies would consistently show it—but they actually show money has little bearing on happiness. If being poor made you unhappy, then people in Indian slums, who live on what they can scavenge, would be the most miserable people in the world—but they're not.

Several studies have been done on being happy and the relationship to money. Picking out some highlights, Princeton did some research published in 2010 that showed that, in the United States, with household earnings up to $75,000 a year, people did get happier as income rose. But above $75,000, it made little or no difference. In other words, once you have enough, having more doesn't make you any happier.

So if you want to be happy in your life, and money isn't going to do the trick (which it won't), what do you do?

Here are some things that the research shows actually make you happy:

- Seeing some value to your life, the hope of achieving something useful, productive, or meaningful to you, and incorporating that value in what you do
- Having a meaning to your life that is greater than just yourself, whether you call it spirituality, vision, or *pay it forward*
- Building relationships and friendships, including helping others less well-off than you
- Activities that use your strengths of character or engage your talents
- Becoming mindful of what you are doing, enjoying now, the only time you have, rather than regretting or gloating over the past, or hoping for or fearing the future

Think of those in terms of Terri and Brad. Terri is going to college to do something she really values. She's excited about becoming an architect and she thinks it's a useful job. It will enable her to design buildings that will benefit people and make them happy. She enjoys it, she wants to study the subject, and she's looking forward to working with other like-minded people. She's going to be doing something she's really interested in and feels she has a natural gift for.

Is it surprising that she's happy and keen to go!

Brad doesn't really know what he values. He doesn't want to disappoint his parents, but he doesn't place a real value on being a CPA either personally or in terms of how he sees himself contributing to society. He doesn't really know what he expects, whether he's going to make new friends in the profession, whether he'll enjoy studying the subject, or whether it's really going to be using his abilities (he's good at math, but there's a lot more to being a CPA than using math).

Is it surprising that he's so uncertain!

Brad may, in fact, really like being a CPA and find it adds great value. But until he sorts through whether it has great value to him in his life and pursuits, it is likely he will be less committed (and less happy) than Terri.

The point is that if you don't know why you're going to college, you're simply not going to have the motivation to overcome the obstacles that everybody has to face in life. You won't want to put in much effort because you don't know whether you'll be happy where you end up, and you certainly won't be very happy working hard to overcome obstacles if you don't care whether you overcome them and aren't having any fun on the way either.

By contrast, if you have a real purpose to going, you have values that will be satisfied, you want to study what you're studying, you feel that you can do something useful, you're going to make friends and build relationships and you're going to make the most of your talents, then it doesn't really matter how tough things get; you'll succeed because you're motivated to overcome any obstacle and you'll be happy doing it.

The obstacles we're concerned with in this book are those involved in planning finances. And it's worth noting that although Brad is talking about being a CPA dealing with money and Terri is talking about architecture looking at buildings, it's Terri who is in a better position to handle her finances. She's the one who is likely to be clear about funding for the optional trips and the extra books and still have a social life. Brad is aware of the end result—*being* a CPA—but not at all clear about how to get there—in large part because he's taking his idea from his parents. So his first step is working out his long-term aims, while Terri can start planning her short-term action plan.

Of course, it's easier if you know exactly what you want at the start. One of my best friends at school decided at the age of four that he wanted to be a physician like his father. He got fantastic grades, got offers from several leading medical schools, had a choice of where he wanted to do his residency, and won prizes—but he was also one of the guys who would party; he was never picked on for being a geek, just admired for being brilliant!

I didn't know what I wanted to do. Most of my friends were going to college, so I thought I might as well go. But I didn't know what I wanted to study. So I went to work instead, went into finance, became a financial advisor, did well at it, was quoted in newspapers, made good money, and one day, in my early 30s, realized that I hated it! It was all about money and subjects such as tax shelters, investment vehicles, life insurance, routine technical solutions—things I was good at but found boring. The bit I found interesting and challenging, finding out about clients' real hopes and desires and dealing with their unique problems, wasn't really rewarded. I got paid most of my money for producing technical solutions that were standard, but that didn't really suit the individual client. I was paid to do the boring stuff, not for what I actually enjoyed and found valuable to me (and to the client). So I went back to college as a mature student and started over!

You can switch like I did, but if you identify those things that really interest you at the start, that you can really have fun doing, that you think are worthwhile, that you get a kick out of, you'll work harder although it may not seem like work and get better results, and not be stymied by obstacles like how to manage your money.

And if what you want to do isn't vocational like accountancy or architecture, that's no problem. I just picked those examples because they're easy to demonstrate. If what you want to do doesn't fit with a particular career, so what? If you do something because people tell you you're good at it, then unless you do enjoy it, it will be hard work, you won't get as good grades, and it won't be of as much use. If you really enjoy it, even if it doesn't have any immediate application, you'll excel at it because you'll work hard at it (although it will seem like fun) and you'll end up with better results and more options.

People (including some career advisers in high schools I've worked with) don't understand that. They tell me that people *should* do practical courses and that college isn't about fun, it's about studying for the future. I agree with them that it's about studying, but why shouldn't it be fun? It's all about motivation, remember.

When I'm doing career advice/coaching, I often get people telling me that they want to do something because it is well paid. The professions are a classic example, as is banking. That's great if you actually want to do what you have to do in that role. But most people who tell me they want to be "a professional" don't really want to do the things the role requires (it is a belief, a guess; they don't really analyze it). They want the money that comes with the role and ignore what you have to do to qualify to get it. So if you don't like reading through pages of detailed, complex documents, how will you get the high-priced lawyer's job? If you don't like the sight of blood, are you really going to make it through 10 years of medical school? And if you do, you may discover that the financial rewards are not enough. Remember the point about the happiness curve—more money doesn't make you happy. All money can do is stop you being unhappy because you can't afford food or a place to live. But once you've got enough for those, money makes very little difference.

Generally, chasing money is not a way to happiness.[1] Materialistic values are likely to make you unhappier, not happier.[2] There's also an increasing amount of evidence that there are three areas where money can help with happiness depending on what you buy with your money. And the evidence is that while buying *things* makes you unhappy, using that money for experiences is one of the ways money can help you to be happier. So **if you've got the money to spare**, an evening with friends, experiencing something new (like flying a plane, learning to drive, or just going to a movie), or visiting a different part of the world can increase your happiness—but buying a plane, a car, a movie studio, or your own island probably won't make you any happier!

Don't get me wrong; there's no problem with having big financial dreams or wanting to be wealthy. So if you really want to do something and the financial rewards for it are tremendous, fantastic. But if it means that you have to spend a lifetime doing something that you don't enjoy, you might want to think about it. Spending 70 hours a week, 50 weeks a year doing something you hate so you can have 2 or 4 weeks' vacation and perhaps a free weekend here or there is actually a recipe for a miserable life.

Think of something you enjoy. It could be anything, math, softball, languages, dancing, making friends, anything. Because you enjoy it, you do it more than most people; you deliberately practice a lot because it's fun. Because you practice a lot, you tend to get good at it. Because you're good at it, you get a sense of mastery, you feel confident and other people notice that you're good and ask you for help. So you do it even more, because that admiration and that sense of mastery is fun. It's a virtuous circle: the more you do it the better you get, the better you get the more fun it is.

Think of something you don't like (which again could be math, softball, languages, dancing, making friends, and so on). You don't like it so you avoid it. Because you avoid it, you don't practice so you don't improve. The only times you do it are when you're forced to, and nobody likes being forced to do things, so you resist it, aren't comfortable, don't enjoy it, and make mistakes. Which possibly starts people teasing you and you hate it even more. It's a vicious circle: the more you hate it the more resistant you are; the more resistant you are the tenser you get; the tenser you get the worse you get and the poorer your performance; and the poorer your performance the more you hate it!

So find out what you want to do, and focus on it being something that you really want to do, whether it is to get to a job you really like or just the course of study for its own sake.

And if you don't know what you want or what will make you happy, we'll look at ways to find out shortly. You can go straight on with looking at what you need to make you happy personally, or you can do some more research about happiness in general.[3]

But first, one warning.

You'll probably have trouble not comparing your money to other peoples', whether it's now, when you're at college or in the future.

"Comparanomics" is what I call measuring wealth (or the lack of it), by comparing ourselves to others. It is why pay rises, lottery wins and so on don't bring any lasting benefit for most people, there's always a different comparison we can make. Look at another example, Ed. Ed is in his middle 30s. For years he's been angling for a promotion. He and Judy, his wife, have planned all the great things they'll do, the vacations, the better home, the bigger car (you get the picture). Finally, Ed gets the promotion and the $50,000 raise. They take a vacation in Europe and meet people who have bigger homes than they do (and *two* vacation homes). They get back and move to a swankier neighborhood. Ed joins the local golf club and soon he has to have special clubs made because everybody else has them and has to buy a Mercedes, because everybody has got one. Meanwhile Judy is meeting the new neighbors, who all have wonderful wardrobes and are all getting their kids riding lessons, tennis lessons and language lessons. And suddenly Ed and Judy realize they need another $50,000 (probably more) to keep feeling as wealthy as before! So more money = feeling poorer, because they don't look at what they've got; they suffer from "comparanomics."

I had that sort of problem when I switched careers. In finance, I earned a lot of money and was paid to be the "expert," the one that colleagues went to for advice, the one the newspapers called for a quote about the latest financial news. When I changed careers, I cut my income to less than 10 percent of what it had been. I was a student—I knew less about psychology than professors who were five or six years younger than me. And I knew that, when I finally qualified, I'd never earn the money I used to in finance (which at the current time is overpaid for the size of the contribution it makes). Industrial and Organizational Psychology (the area I studied) is recurrently undervalued for its contribution.

People I've told about this (and my friends and family at the time) are equally divided in opinion between, "that was wonderful, I wish I'd been that brave instead of sticking with the boring job I've got" and "you're crazy, you gave up a well-paid job to do psychology, you need your head examined!" I put aside my *status* as an expert and the big money and became a student again and relatively poor. But I studied something I found fascinating, did all the optional reading, worked really hard (although I was just having fun), came out with a distinction in my postgrad work, got my qualification as fast as it's possible to do it, and after that I got to spend my time doing something I really enjoy, so I'm far happier!

Wanting big financial reward is not a bad thing. If it is really going to make you happy, and it really is for you, great. Good luck to you. But if you have to force yourself to study something you hate for 4 years to be able to do a job you hate for 40 years to be able to buy a Mustang because a guy in the dorm room bought a Corvette, that's crazy. If you're going to do something you love, or you always wanted a Mustang, it is your dream and you plan how to afford it, that's fine.

In the course of this book, I hope we can shift from "comparanomics" to have you focus on what drives you. Ideally, you just do what you really want to do to be happy and not worry about what other people think.

Let's look at some ways to find what you really want to be happy, to make sure you've got the motivation, the "why" to go after what you really want and forget about what other people think.

If you don't really know what you want, try one or more of these exercises:

• Imagine you're 10 years older, have finished college, started a career, and are being interviewed on a TV program. Imagine it's your favorite interviewer (Oprah, Jon Stewart, Ellen DeGeneres). What do you tell them about you, the achievements you are most proud of, memories you recall the most fondly?

- Imagine that you are totally free of obligations. Who would you give money to, what charities would you support, what relatives or friends would you invest in, what businesses or foundations would you start?
- What is your perfect life? Where would you go and what things would you spend your time doing? What would you do with your time, how you would live, who you would mix with, what would you want to achieve?

You might find it useful to try this with a trusted friend or relative. Or it might be something that you want to do privately. It doesn't matter; the idea is to get you thinking about what is really important to you. When you open up your mind to what you really want to achieve, feel you could be proud of, and would do if you had the chance, then you're on the way toward creating the chance to achieve it.

In the same way, you can think about the second point about things that build happiness, having a meaning to your life that is greater than just yourself.

Do you volunteer in a Big Brother or Big Sister Program? Do you do any coaching, act as a summer camp counselor, coach sports or help the less fortunate? You might have thought about this earlier, thought about a charity that you'd start, maybe because you've got a friend or relative who has been struck by some disease or problem. It's a proven fact that spending time doing something that benefits others is a great way to feel happier—and obviously, it has a huge benefit to society as a whole. It might seem strange that it makes you feel happy, but if you do something like that and think about the feeling you get from it, you'll know what I mean. And if you don't, talk to people who do and you'll get the idea. The fact is that human beings are social animals. We want to help others, and the historical reason for it is because it was a useful tribal bond and it meant that if we were in trouble, people would help us as well. So we all evolved to get a good feeling from helping others; it is a survival characteristic that prompts us to cooperate and be social. It's one reason why solitary confinement is a punishment; being unable to have human contact, to help and be helped, ultimately becomes a torture.

This is also the second of the three areas where spending money *can* (to an extent) buy happiness. If you spend money on others, it can help you be happier. If you spend on yourself, it probably won't make much difference. There's scientific evidence to back up the fact that it is better to give than to receive—in terms of happiness.[4]

A third point that helps with happiness is building relationships and friendships. We've already mentioned helping people who are less well-off, but what about just having good relationships?

Something that you can do is to think about what you enjoy:

Job?
School?
Hobbies?
Computer games (multi- or sole player)?
Reading?
Time with your friends and/or family?

If some of those are things you enjoy, chances are they break down into two types. One type is based on activities that allow you to socialize. Maybe you spend a lot of time on Facebook, keeping up with friends; maybe you meet regularly or spend time texting. These activities feed the human desire for contact, to be connected to other people, to be a social animal.

The second type of activities that most people tend to enjoy, like solo computer games, reading, and so on, sound as if they're the opposite; they're things you do on your own. But they reflect another source of happiness, activities that use your strengths of character or engage your real interests. So you might be reading magazines and books about your interests, playing computer games that engage your wits or reactions, or having hobbies that engage your talents.

Think about the things you really enjoy. And look at why you enjoy them. I'm prepared to bet that 99 percent of what you want to do is either involved with social bonds, or it allows you to engage in things that you feel you have a talent for, or a real interest in that you want to develop a talent for.

I won't try to give you relationship advice, except to say that if you think that you'll be happy in isolation and don't want any relationships with other people, you're probably wrong. People really do need people and it's very unusual for anybody to be truly happy when they're always isolated. So when you're looking at what you want to do with your life (and your college studies) to be happy, you almost certainly want to make sure you build in time with friends, old and new.

With talents, character strengths and activities to engage your interest, I can give you more advice. You might know what you're good at; maybe you find it easy to talk to people and make friends or you are the one people look to as a leader. Maybe you are the one they bring their problems to because you're a great listener. Everybody has talents. Sometimes, like most people from time to time (particularly in teenage years), you might feel that you don't have anything anybody admires, but you do.

One way you can check this out is to take a survey about character strengths. There are various ones around, but an especially useful one is called VIA for Values in Action (www.viacharacter.org).

What the survey results will tell you is a good starting point. It's not the whole answer, but they will give you a base to start thinking about "what do I really want to do with my life; what talents do I want to use that are likely to make me happy in what I do."

That covers a lot of the areas that are likely to make you happy. If you're not like Terri or my friend Tim and don't know what you want to do in life, aren't sure what course is right for you, or aren't sure if you're making the right decisions, you've got something to work with.

Let's go back to Brad now. He didn't really know. So he and I looked at what he saw his ideal life being like, did a mock TV interview, and so on (as I described earlier, with me pretending to be Oprah!). He found he really dreamed about being involved in entertainment, not necessarily as a performer, but he thought about the producers and technical people he'd seen interviewed and was really excited by the idea of one day being involved and telling stories about that.

We looked at his strengths and three that came out were creativity, judgment and perseverance. In other words, he would tend to stick to something he thought was worthwhile after most people would give up, he was good at analyzing and critical thinking, and he was creative. So that suggested that he'd be very good at dealing with problems, because he could analyze them, try to solve them, keep trying, and if one way didn't work come up with a creative approach instead of just hammering away at it in the same way.

Brad was starting to get interested—he was pretty typical in that, while he'd put on a brave front he was actually pretty scared that he wasn't good enough. What he was seeing was somebody who had a lot of potential, but he still wasn't quite sure what he could do with that potential.

So we looked at some of the other "happiness" points. Relationships weren't a big issue; he got on well with his family, had great friends, and was confident that he'd get on with people whatever he did; and he wouldn't be lonely or isolated. But when we looked at *social value*, something clicked into place. He loved documentary films, the kind that open people's eyes to the world around them.

At this point he'd got some choices. Maybe he wants to go for something in the film school line—he's certainly got the intelligence and creativity for it. He could even please his parents and train for a financial role, with the intention of going into documentary film making—after all, how do you think budgets get raised without producers who are creative, persevering, analytical, good with people and who genuinely believe in what they're doing and its value? But instead of just leaping in and saying "yes, I'll study accountancy and specialize in film," he could now research it. He could talk to people who made documentary films, find out how they got funding, what knowledge you needed to be successful, how creative it was feasible to be, what sort of obstacles you had to overcome, what it took to be a producer, and whether you could move from the pure accounts side. Then, when he knew, if he still liked the idea, he could look at which colleges offered the courses he would need, where they were, how long the courses were, what the fees were, whether they had links to production companies, and so on.

So he was heading into the same territory as Terri; he was developing a real motivation, a "why" that would carry him on.

Hopefully that gives you an idea of what you can do, if you aren't sure at the moment what you want from college. And hopefully it's becoming clearer why that first question "why are you going to college" is so important.

Maybe, also, you noticed that one of those elements of happiness I mentioned initially didn't get into the story so far. It was the point about being mindful.

It hasn't come up so far for two reasons.

First, it didn't really matter with Brad or with Terri up to the points we've taken their stories. Not that it might not have helped them, but it wasn't vital to either of them so far.

Second, it tends to be really helpful when you need to make important decisions without impulses and emotions getting in the way. That's a reason why a lot of major businesses are starting to get interested and getting their executives and staff to practice mindfulness. Examples are Google, Aetna, General Mills, AOL, Time Warner, and Target. Sometimes the initial idea is to help people control stress and be able to work without burnout. However, as they learn more about it, organizations are realizing it makes a difference to the quality of the decisions people make. Even the US military has seen the benefits, despite a common perception that the military (like big business) would laugh at something that seems so "freaky." The fact is that it works, and the military and businesses are dedicated to things that work. Try looking up the *Washington Times* article, "Marines expanding use of meditation training," and hunt out some of the large corporate projects. You'll find that training your mind in this way is at the cutting edge of modern business and military thinking, because it really works to help make better decisions.

I'll suggest some ways to start using mindfulness for yourself in a moment, but one of the times when you might find it hardest to make decisions or even to think straight is if you're depressed or stressed. And it can be pretty stressful trying to work out about college, your finances, and your future. By the way, there are some useful resources for getting through that stress, and some of them are free.[5]

You might be thinking "I'm not unhappy or depressed, I don't need this mindfulness." But stay with me here: Imagine you're trying to make choices about what you're doing, how to afford it, and so on. You're thinking "what will my parents say, what am I going to do with my life, where are my friends going, is it better to get into something where I'll make money or to do what I really want which probably won't lead to a job," and so on. It's easy for your head to be so full of ideas that you don't know what you're doing. One day you think one way, the next another. You talk to your parents, to your high-school teacher, and to some friends and each time you're convinced they're right (or wrong), and when you speak to the next one, you change your mind again.

This is where mindfulness can help: to be able to relieve the pressure, block out the "noise," slow down, and work out what you really think.

Let's meet Paul. He hasn't done much thinking about college yet. He's got plenty of other worries that are filling his mind. He has a test tomorrow and is wondering whether he's prepared enough, what his parents will say when they find out about him getting a tattoo, whether his girlfriend is going to like the surprise he's planned for her birthday next week. He's busy worrying about what is going to happen, or might happen, in future. He's also worrying about what he did at the party last weekend and whether his tutor will find out, whether what he said to the coach about the game was going to get him into trouble, and if his buddies not telling him about the concert tickets first means they don't want to include him. Again, his mind is full of regrets or worries from the past, instead of about what he's doing now.

And here's the thing: The human body doesn't really know what's real and what's imagination. So Paul's body is ready for action, his pulse rate is speeding up, he's got more sugar in his bloodstream, he's all set to fight or run—because of what's going on in his head and there's no *physical* threat to fight off. So he's burning a lot of energy and has got a lot of chemicals in his system that are fine for a short period (like making a big play in the game) but will hurt him if they stay there for days with him worrying and just spinning his wheels.

He's also got a mind full of worries, dreading tomorrow or regretting yesterday, and he can't focus on what he wants to do right now, like work out what to do about college and how to pay for it.

Put very simply, mindfulness is about getting away from the past and the future and being conscious of right now.

I've given you a book and website in the endnotes, but if you want a quick guide, try it out for yourself.

Find a time when you can make sure you won't be interrupted. Ten minutes or so will do to start with; you can always build it up later.

Turn your phone off or onto silent and make sure you can let the world go for that time, or you'll constantly be wondering who is calling, what you "should" be doing, and so on. I usually set a timer so I'm not going to be worried that I'll fall asleep or something.

Sit, in a chair or on a cushion, or lie down, with your body symmetrical (so, have your legs uncrossed, don't twist round, and so on). You can have your eyes closed or open, whatever suits you best. Let your spine be straight, without straining, and if you're sitting, let your head balance on the top of your neck with as little tension as possible.

Let your hands rest in your lap, or at your sides.

Then focus on what's happening right now. That can be being aware of your breath—feel the air as it goes in and out of your nose, or as it makes your belly rise and fall. You can focus on the feel of your feet on the ground, your arms touching your lap (or the floor, bed, or whatever), or on the weight of your body being supported on your back or buttocks.

You can listen to the sounds around you, noises in the distance or the sound of your breath. You can just be aware of your thoughts as they come and go. You can count your breaths if you find that helpful or just focus on the feeling. If you're counting, count in, out, 1, in, out 2, and so on up to 10, then start again at 1. It's not to prove anything, simply to give you something to focus on if you find that the breath, your weight on the seat, or whatever is not enough and your mind keeps wandering.

The point is just to be, not to do. Just observe. You don't have to do anything, change anything, accomplish anything. You just observe your breath, the sense of touch, of hearing, your thoughts or whatever it is you're focusing on.

You'll almost certainly find your mind wanders. That's no problem; that's what minds do. It's normal. When you notice it's wandered, don't give yourself a hard time; just bring it back to your breath or whatever you're focusing on. It's great that you noticed, it means that you're focused "in the moment" and it's a sign that you're mindful of what's going on. Just bring it back gently to whatever you're focused on and carry on.

It will probably feel as if, as you try to relax and let your mind settle, thoughts come crowding in and it feels like your head has become Grand Central in the rush hour. Don't worry; that's normal; it's just because you're realizing all the thoughts that are crashing around all the time but that normally you don't notice. The best analogy I've heard is that your mind is like a waterfall. Thoughts are flooding down and it seems like it's all noise and confusion. But if you can let that happen, you'll increasingly find that your mind calms down and becomes like the pool downstream that is calm and peaceful. That calmness, the clarity that you get (probably only for a few seconds at a time to start with), is what is great to deal with stress and pressure, and it's one of the reasons that meditating regularly helps you to think more clearly.

You don't have to *try* to do anything. Just allow yourself to be "in the moment" and observe whatever is there in that moment.

It sounds ridiculously simple, but it is surprisingly hard to do; we're all so used to being busy, to be doing things all the time.

And it is a proven way to reduce stress and to allow you to escape from the "overwhelming" feeling of having too many ideas, too many pressures, too much choice. So stick with it, and perhaps try some guided meditations (from CDs or the Internet), which are a help.

Now if we go back to Paul, because his mind was buzzing like a hive of bees, teaching him some basics of mindfulness allowed him to quieten his mind down. He might still worry about the test, his parents' or his girlfriend's reaction, what his buddies meant, and so on. But he started to be able to get more emotional distance from it. He was able to discuss worries with me without constantly breaking off to say "and there's this as well" he could put things in perspective. And that meant he wasn't so stressed and had the energy to start thinking about college.

Oddly, the third of the three ways to spend money to "buy" happiness is not to spend money at the moment you want to. Research shows you get more happiness from waiting and anticipating spending, than you do from impulsive spending now. It's counterintuitive, it feels like the thing that "I've got to have" that you buy is a real buzz, but actually it gives you a lot less than anticipating getting it, leaving it a while, contemplating it, and then buying it. And, of course, you might find you don't want it after all, so you get all the fun of anticipation and haven't spent any money!

Now, let's return to my first point—make sure you know the answer to why you're going to college.

What is it that you want from the experience?

What things make you happy, and are you going to get them from what you're planning to do?

Do you have values, a purpose that you can see that you really want to achieve?

Do you have particular strengths or interests that you can use?

Can you enjoy the time now (and your time on the course)?

If you're going to spend money, can you spend at least part of it on experiences rather than "things" or on others rather than yourself, and can you contemplate and anticipate rather than spend impulsively?

If you've got those things worked out, you're probably going to enjoy and do well at college. You've got the motivation, and you've got a very good idea of what you want your money to do for you.

## SUMMARY

You are more important and more complex than money. So focus on you.

"Why" is more powerful than "how"; motives are what drive the world, not methods.

If you want to live happily, find out what really does it for you—it won't be having "things."

Try the exercises, websites, and so on to find out what you value, your strengths, and other ideas that will help you be happy.

Try mindfulness; it is a help to clear thinking.

## NOTES

1. Deepak Chopra, "A Very Bad Idea That Millions of People Believe" (accessed 4/19/14) https://www.linkedin.com/today/post/article/20140403012 255-75054000-a-very-bad-idea-that-millions-of-people-believe?trk=mta-lnk&utm _content=bufferff036&utm_medium=social&utm_source=linkedin.com&utm _campaign=buffer

2. Tim Kasser, *The High Price of Materialism* (London: MIT Press, 2002).

3. If you want to look at the research for yourself, rather than take my short cuts, there's plenty of good information about the subject of happiness. Some well-researched scientific works that are also highly accessible include Martin Seligman's *Authentic Happiness Using the New Positive Psychology to Realize Your Potential for Deep Fulfillment* (London: Nicholas Brealey Publishing,

2003), Ed Diener and Robert Biswas-Diener's *Happiness: Unlocking the Mysteries of Psychological Wealth* (Malden, MA: Wiley-Blackwell, 2008), and Matthieu Ricard's *Happiness: A Guide to Developing Life's Most Important Skill* (London: Atlantic Books, 2007). Also helpful is Viktor Frankl's *Man's Search for Meaning* (London: Rider, 2004).

4. Elizabeth Dunn et al., "Spending Money on Others Promotes Happiness" *Science* 119 (2008), 1687–1688.

5. There's a great book called, *The Mindful Way Through Depression: Freeing Yourself from Chronic Unhappiness* (New York: Guilford Press, 2007) by Williams, Teasdale, Segal, and Kabat-Zinn that is designed to help you; it's even got a CD of guided practices to work with. The practice of mindfulness tends to help people to put aside pressure and be able to focus (you need not be depressed to begin mindfulness practice!). Another resource is the University of Auckland site http://www.calm.auckland.ac.nz/18.html, which has a whole series of different free mindfulness and other meditation downloads.

Chapter 2

# What Does Money Mean to You?

What do you think about money: is it good, bad, important, trivial?

That (again) probably sounds like a silly question. Everybody likes money, right?

But some people break the law for it, kill, steal, break various commandments, risk their health, their reputation, their family or their lives for it, and envy those who have more. Would you do those things? Do you like it that much? Some regard money with suspicion, distrust those with money, and would rather not be tainted by having it. Is that you? Some think it's evil; as it says in the King James Bible, "It is easier for a camel to go through the eye of a needle, than for a rich man to enter into the kingdom of God." Do you think that's true? And some see money as one tool in their toolkit, to be used with other tools (education, initiative, community) to get them where they want to go. Is that you?

We all have beliefs, our own "money story" that we tell ourselves whenever we think about money. Our money stories are largely based on emotion and habit and are shaped by our experience. If the conversation about money **always** generated an argument in your family growing up, your brain has a well-worn path away from talking or thinking about money, to avoid trouble. If, on the other hand, your parents taught you to be resourceful, talked openly about money as a tool and you always felt there was "enough" (no matter whether you were "rich" or "poor" by government measures), your level of stress around money is likely to be low. It's important to know what your own emotions and habits are and whether they are still relevant and useful to you. And now is a terrific time to think about rewriting your story: You are "breaking out" in all kinds of ways—so much has changed about money and life since your parents were 20!

Having talked in the last chapter about where you want to get to, in this chapter, we'll look at where you are at the moment. You always need to know where you **are** to navigate from there to where you are **going**! But first, let's take a little side trip.

## YOUR BRAINPOWER

As human beings, we have the ability to reason, which makes us intelligent, rational beings, so we'd expect to be able to make intelligent, rational choices and not be governed by habit and emotion. But that's not as easy as it sounds!

The human brain is the most complex single thing in the known universe. It has phenomenal abilities. Because it's so powerful, it needs a lot of fuel. It only makes up about 2 percent of our body weight but uses about 15 percent of the blood flow, 20 percent of the oxygen, and 25 percent of the glucose used by the whole body. Naturally, the brain works to process things as efficiently as possible and develops neural paths that exhibit as habits so it can save energy. Have you ever injured the hand you write with and tried to teach yourself to write with the other hand? Exhausting, isn't it? Your brain is creating a new neural pathway, but until it's 'set', each thought and action is processed individually and consciously, which takes a lot of energy.

The same is true around emotions: Your brain has a basic, and very strong, "fight or flight" response to save energy on thinking under pressure. Even if you are an optimist, you are ready to fight or run when you feel threatened (physically or otherwise). This response can be altered, but you need to be aware of it before you can alter it.

## MONEY STORIES

Now, back to the money story—an example. When Angela and her brother were young (Angela was 10; her brother was 8), their father lost his job. He was made redundant—which was going to mean a **significant** change in their lifestyle. One of the core values (remember from Chapter 1) Angela's parents had was family, and money was a tool for supporting family. So what to do now? They called a family meeting and explained what was going on and that everyone would have to be more resourceful going forward, but that they were all in it together. Angela took it to heart and did what she could to contribute and, along the way, became very resourceful. When she received compliments for her dressing style, she took pleasure in the fact that she was able to stand out—at bargain prices by shopping in sales and consignment boutiques. She was also grateful to her parents for being transparent and including her and her brother in a difficult conversation and conveying the responsibility expected of each family member. The family had monthly "money" meetings, and each month a different family member chaired the meeting and was responsible for developing an agenda. So Angela's money story was based on the values of family and responsibility, and because the family continued the practice of talking about money, reviewing her situation and the resources available became Angela's habit. And her story developed over time: She learned new things so her "pathways" were not fixed; they were flexible.

We all learned in our past to react in certain ways—by observing those around us and by real experiences (you don't put your hand on a hot stove twice!). From these, the brain develops neural pathways, or habits, in order to conserve energy. That instinctive system of forming habits and pathways is more fuel efficient and faster than thinking each situation through each time.

Those pathways are really helpful most of the time, but once our brain has a way to respond to a situation that it finds works, it will apply it rather than making up new responses for each new situation. That can mean we never bother to look for new, more useful, pathways to get to new places we want to go. If we stick with the automatic habits, the old money story, and the familiar paths, our economical shortcut can become a long way round to our new destination.

So as we get older it is useful to check every once in a while, as Angela did, to make sure that the story the brain has developed is useful for what we want now. And if it's not useful, develop new paths, new habits, and rewrite our money story.

Checking your story and seeing whether your habits are helpful in your particular situation, or not, allow you freedom. Without "unpacking" your story, you may be stuck in a very limited range of behaviors; some of which will impede your progress in adulthood and particularly in handling your money.

To start you on some of that unpacking, here's an exercise you can try (this works best in groups, but give it a try on your own and then try it out as a game when you are hanging out with friends). Each person or team gets a sheet of paper. On one complete the sentence, "Rich people are _____." On the other, complete the sentence, "Poor people are _____." Take five minutes to think of as many adjectives as possible and write them down. Then you collect the papers.

Now compare the answers on the two sheets and circle the words that are the same on both. What I usually find is at least a 50 percent overlap. In other words what you may say about rich people—they're lazy, virtuous, greedy, workaholics—your colleague(s) say(s) about poor people!

You might think "I know that having a view like 'poor people are X; rich people are Y' is just an opinion, not a fact that I'd be able to support with evidence." That's certainly what I thought when I first studied it.

But it isn't as easy as that! The "go to" thinking you've established comes up as your first reaction, which sets in motion a series of thoughts—your brain on autopilot! Here's a different example.

Imagine that you are helping out with teaching at a local junior school. You split the children into two groups by their eye color. The blue eyed can only break for recess after the brown eyed have left, and the blue eyed can't speak to the superior brown eyed until they're spoken to. Would you be surprised if the brown eyed became more confident and the blue eyed more frightened and submissive? How about if the brown eyed's reading and writing abilities markedly improved and the blue eyed's abilities got worse? What about if, the next day, you reversed it and told them that blue eyed were superior? Do you think that the results would reverse or that a spelling test would show that each group's spelling ability altered depending on whether they were told they were superior?

It's been done, and the results do work like that. An authority figure telling people something makes people "live up" to the expectation. And it doesn't matter whether it's something that is definitely not true—eye color has absolutely no influence on reading, writing or spelling ability, nor is there any reason for confidence to change because of eye color.

If we humans were logical, we'd analyze the situation and reason that eye color doesn't affect intelligence, and the experiment wouldn't produce those results. But we don't reason like that. Unless we deliberately think about it, our brains accept the statement unconsciously and our behavior changes accordingly. Hence the children behaved as if eye color *does* affect intelligence. And if those statements go on long enough, and we never question them (even if they are ridiculous), then our brains set up pathways and habits accordingly. Your money story, the one you repeat to yourself any time you think about money, could be the most nonsensical statement in the world, but if you don't question it you'll probably end up with habits that are based on it being true. So, if your money story is, "I'm not good at managing money," it is almost certainly going to influence you. You'll try to live up (or down) to the expectation, even if it's nonsense and actually you're a financial genius!

The most obvious influences on your money story are the systems around you. The closest and most influential system is your family system, influenced, in turn, by a cultural system, in tandem with institutional systems (school, job, government). I am not here to advocate that you need to **change** those larger systems but that you be aware of the role the systems play in developing, and rewriting, your money story. In this way you will be able to focus on those things in your money story that you **can** change.

We'll look at how you get influenced by the "system dynamic" (e.g., your family) in your life in just a minute. But for the moment, let's think about some *types* of behavior around money.

### Types of Behavior

We want to hold these up and look at them, and what we could do is be very scientific about it. But that isn't much fun—we all like stories, remember!

So let me tell you a story, and because most people like animals, I'll make it about animals.

I've always loved animals, and we have four cats (this is true, by the way). There's Luciano, the world's only Buddhist cat, who never hunts and loves everything and everybody, only eats because he has to, and would be vegetarian if he could. There's Lucy, who hunts for the fun of hunting. She will catch a mouse or bird and play with it; if it won't run, she'll hit it until it does so she can catch it again. If it dies, it is by accident and she loses interest; she never eats it or kills it deliberately. If we find something dead with no mark on it, it was Lucy caught it. Leopold hunts to kill things; he's been known to take a bird on the wing and kill it as he hits the ground. He never eats them or plays with them. If we find it dead with a broken neck or throat bite, it was Leopold caught it. Demelza hunts to eat; she doesn't play with food or walk away from the body. If we find some feet, a beak, or the little wobbly bit (gall bladder?), it was Demelza caught it.

Three of the cats do what cats do. They show different bits of the urge to hunt; one hunts only, one hunts to kill and one hunts to eat, but none of them actually need to do any of it. They do it because they are driven to it by urges they don't understand. That's OK; they're cats. The fact that there is no need for the behavior and in two out of three cases it isn't actually a functional behavior doesn't matter. But if we apply it to people, it's a bit different.

People have a mind that can examine those habits, beliefs and money stories. We're not confined to doing what our habits or instincts say we *should* do. That's what Angela does (remember Angela?); she can decide for herself what she wants, and whether her thinking and her actions are working for her.

Luciano is a very unusual cat; he doesn't appear to need to do "cat things" just because he is a cat. He behaves like a mature human, like Angela. He makes up his mind about what he thinks is worth doing and doesn't seem to care what people (or cats!) think cats *ought* to do, what other cats do or what his ancestors thousands of years ago *had* to do.

If you unpack your money story, you can do the same thing. If you don't, you might be lucky and it will work out OK for you. But it might not. You might be like one of the other cats.

Lucy has to hunt. She doesn't get any food out of it; she just follows the cat hunting instinct. Once she's done that, she doesn't really know what to do next, so she'll keep playing with the prey and pretend to hunt it until it dies or gets away. She isn't flexible; she just keeps repeating the same action, like people who shop (or spend money in other ways) and waste money and energy doing something that isn't of any use. It typifies people who do something because that's what they've always done (so it's the triumph of the money story over the life they want). It's OK for a cat; Lucy is perfectly happy and a lovely cat. But it's not so helpful for a human.

Leopold hunts just as much. He also doesn't get food; he has a desire to kill the prey but then loses interest. He also isn't flexible; he can't keep from looking for the next kill, which is what cats do, and he's a wonderful cat. But with people, behaving like that is typical of the person who always wants to have the newest, latest, most fashionable model. They might be the victim of stereotypes (the geek, the blonde, the jock, and so on) and/or be a person who does things because other people do and doesn't bother to think what she or he really wants. Leopold is a happy cat and what he does is fine, for a cat. But a human who is stuck in a stereotype or wants things because other people want them, and not because they are really valuable to the person her or himself, is likely to be stuck in behavior that is not going to make him or her happy.

Demelza hunts as well and she does get food for it. She doesn't actually need the food; all the cats get a good diet and they're very healthy. In fact they are considerably healthier (and longer lived) than feral cats. What she does is fine for a cat. But lots of people act like her; they obsessively chase money whether they need it or not. She wants to have food she doesn't need, mainly because she's driven by being a hunter. That's OK; she's a cat and she doesn't have a big human brain (but we love her anyway). But how many people have the *need* to prove they are rich or powerful and chase something that doesn't make them happy, in fact, spend their life making themselves (and their loved ones) unhappy? Remember in Chapter 1 how happiness is linked to values and activities that matter and not money and that a drive to having material things is linked to being unhappy.

So if you are like Luciano (and Angela) and happy that you are flexible and can adapt your money behavior to whatever you want, you can skip to the next chapter right now. But if you are like Leopold, Lucy, or Demelza and see it might be useful to adapt some of your habits, to change your money story so you can use your money to help you better, what do you do?

## FLEXIBLE BEHAVIOR

The first thing is to experiment with small changes. Going for a wholesale change will confuse you, remember the pathways concept and how complex your brain is. Trying to make massive changes to all your habits at once would be like trying to rewire a major city, solo, overnight!

So ask yourself, "what is a small change I can make in the way I handle money that will move me toward where I want to go?"

For example, Mark knew, roughly, what his expenses were every month and he wasn't really interested in budgeting (it made him feel confined). But he knew two things: There wasn't much left over at the end of the month, and he did want to go to Paris on his spring holiday. He had three main choices: just go, put the trip on a credit card, and worry about it later; experiment with saving the money specifically for the trip; or ask his parents to pay for the trip. His *normal* way would have been to go on the trip and worry about paying for it later. But he decided to experiment with a different way. So, what did he need to know? He needed to know at least two things: How much the trip was going to cost and what spending choices he had to make in order to save the money for the trip in the time he had (fortunately, he had six months)?

We'll look at how Mark set up the goals and what he did later. But he realized that the way he'd always behaved in the past—not knowing what he really wanted (if he'd known, he'd have made sure he had money at the end of the month for it) and not really planning his finances and budgeting—wasn't going to work for him now.

Mark's situation was pretty simple. He didn't really need to think much about his "money story." He just had to think about what he could do differently. Take a more complicated (but still very common) example.

Jenny comes from a family that's very loving, but that has very clear ideas about what is "ladylike." Her money story includes the belief that women are not good at math (which isn't true; there's no gender difference in math ability), that it is somehow not right for women to be concerned with money and business and that they should leave it to men. That isn't true either; it might be the way her parents do it, it might be what they believe, but there isn't any fact to back it up. It's just something that everybody in the family takes to be true.

Because she's grown up believing it's true, Jenny's money story includes the "facts" that it's too complicated for her and that it wouldn't be appropriate for her, as a lady, to be concerned about spending or budgeting—and it certainly wouldn't be appropriate for her to *talk* about it! Consequently she not only has the habit of letting her parents provide her with money and pay the bills, but she has little experience with money for herself. She's never had to take the consequences of, for example, not having a phone because she couldn't pay the bill or faced the humiliation of taking an impulse buy back to the shop because she couldn't afford it.

That might sound great; buy things and mum and dad will bail you out! But it is a huge problem, because one day Jenny will have to fend for herself. Whether it's when she goes to college, when she becomes a parent herself or when she lives on her own, one day, she will have to deal with money. And trying to do that for the first time if, for example, she's a widow with a couple of young children and has plenty of other problems without being totally unable to handle or even think about money, well, that's not a good time to start learning.

Jenny's parents thought they were helping her, taking the pressure off her and teaching her to be a lady. They had the best intentions, but the money story Jenny has won't help her at all when she's about to go to college.

That makes Jenny's situation more complex than Mark's. It's not just a case of doing something different. Jenny needs to think about what her story is, unpack it, and think about what's real and what's just a belief that used to be convenient but now doesn't work, like a pathway that is well used but heads in the wrong direction.

Doing that unpacking is particularly difficult for her for two reasons. It takes effort to challenge your story, to alter your habits and cut new pathways (remember the point about learning to write with your other hand). And she doesn't want to argue with her parents or upset them; she knows they only did what they thought was right. In both cases, Jenny is stepping out of a safely worn path and her brain's response is to go on the defensive.

So she needs a way to help her change her own story and to make that change acceptable to her parents.

With Jenny (and other clients in similar situations) I suggest two things. One we've talked about, mindfulness. When she started to be able mentally to "step back" from the situation, Jenny became clearer about what she needed to do. She also found she was calmer and more able to think about how she could communicate to her parents about taking responsibility for herself without upsetting them or being (in their minds) unladylike.

The other was something based on Cognitive Behavioral Coaching (CBC). Essentially, it's a way of coaching people that is based on something else we've talked about; that the way you think (e.g., your *story* and your beliefs) affects the way you feel and, consequently, your actions (e.g., your behaviors/habits). So there's a link between thought (Cognition) and Behavior, and the Coaching is to help understand that link and to make it work for you. The idea is to identify what triggers the story, to unpack it, to see whether it's working for you, and, if not, to develop small ways to change your reaction.

It's easy to remember, because it starts with ABC. That stands for **Activating** event, **Beliefs**, and **Consequences**, emotional or behavioral.

What you add is D and E, which stands for **Dispute** and **Effective** outlook.

Let's look at how that worked with Jenny.

The **activating** event might be something like seeing a new dress that would be great for a party Jenny was going to but that had a price tag higher than she would normally spend.

Her **belief** would be that she couldn't really deal with working out the finance. And it wouldn't be ladylike to buy a cheaper dress or perhaps adapt something in her closet and add some accessories.

The **consequences** behaviorally would be that Jenny would buy the dress. She'd know that she could explain to her mother how important it was to have something new, how she couldn't possibly be *cheap*, how it wasn't ladylike to adapt old clothes. And she knew that, however angry her father might be over her spending so much hard-earned money, she could play the "helpless girl bewildered by the male financial world" card, and he would pay up. The consequences emotionally were that she reinforced the belief that she couldn't handle money and that being helpless and dependent were somehow more valuable than being adult and making her own decisions. Ironically, it also meant that all her brain's energy, which she might have applied to handling her money, went into working out how to handle her parents and behaving in a way that kept her dependent and not responsible. It meant she was behaving like one of the cats—automatically doing what she'd always done.

What we did was to get Jenny to pick it up at A, the **activating** event. When she had a situation like that, where the **belief** was triggered, she started to **dispute** the belief.

The thinking went something like this, "why shouldn't I be able to handle money. I get good grades and I'm going to college. And money is pretty simple actually. I can work out how to handle people, like my parents; they're much more complicated. $1 and $1 are always $2, but put two people together—like my mum and dad—and you get all sorts of different results. And why isn't it ladylike to be good with money? There are *Fortune* Magazine lists of female executives and the lowest one listed makes over $10 million a year. I'd like to see somebody tell them that they aren't ladylike."

That could give Jenny an **effective** outlook, such as "I'm going to learn more about money and to start with I'm going to take responsibility for what I spend, so I won't waste money on that dress unless I'm sure I can afford it. A lady is a grown up, and grown ups are responsible for the consequences of what they do while a child has to be looked after, so it's more ladylike to take responsibility."

There were lots of similar disputes that we worked on. Jenny, for example, researched successful women and found out what advice they gave to aspiring business women and, in the process, gained several role models that were feminine and ladylike enough to wow her mother, while having top-notch business and finance brains that really impressed her father!

The sort of disputes you might produce would probably be based on similar challenges to the beliefs you've got. Examples are:

*Is this thought true? What is your evidence for it?* With Jenny, the beliefs she had fell apart when examined in the light of evidence.

*Does one example of something mean it is always the case?* If Jenny felt negative, she might think about the time she ran up a huge cell phone bill and her father told her that this proved she couldn't handle money.

But there were plenty of examples of where she could handle it, and bearing in mind that she had very little experience, and had never been given much opportunity, she was actually very good.

*What other explanations are there for the situation? Are they more realistic?* Jenny would, in the past, have run up bills that her father would end up paying. That might be because Jenny was "no good" with money. But other explanations include that her parents had convinced her that she wasn't and therefore she didn't even try, that she had been encouraged to avoid handling money so when she had to think about it, she didn't have much experience to work from, and that she was told effectively that handling money was unladylike and therefore she shouldn't do it. It's far more likely that her behavior was less about her ability and more about her false beliefs.

*If one of your friends thought like this, would you judge him or her the same way? What would you advise her or him to do or to think that you're not telling yourself?* Jenny's not really in that position, but a lot of people, being told that they are "no good with money," believe it and think it's their fault. They mentally beat themselves up for being stupid. And, of course, that is pretty depressing, so often they want to go and get some "retail therapy" to make themselves feel better! And then they have another piece of "evidence" for being no good with money; it's a vicious circle. Jenny would sympathize with a friend like that and probably tell her or him that it hadn't been their fault, but while they couldn't change the past, it was now time to take responsibility for the future. If you're in the situation where you're beating yourself up over problems with money, what would you tell a friend who came to you with the same problem?

*Does this belief, even if it is true, help you in any way to be the person you want to be?* Jenny was very clear that neither her existing view of being "no good with money" nor it being "unladylike" to be good with money was true. But even if she felt her view had been true, she could check whether it would help her. You might have that situation. You might have some experience with budgeting, for example, trying to pay your phone bill out of your allowance. And you might have failed miserably and had to ask for help to pay the bill as you really need the phone. And maybe you've been told that shows you're no good with money. And at the moment, it might be true; maybe you aren't Warren Buffett yet. But does it help you to believe that you're not good with money and that you never will be? Will it help you be what you want to be and get where you want to get? I want you to think about what beliefs are going to help you. Maybe you can think, "OK, I'm not that great yet and I don't have a good track record, but that view isn't going to help me. I need to learn, and I've been successful at learning other things, I'm smart, and I want to learn this so that I can be the person I want to be, be independent, go to college, and accomplish things. I can change, I'm not fixed forever in one way of behaving." You may be tempted to believe that you were absent when everyone received a copy of "The Money Rulebook," but learning how to handle money is like learning how to drive: There are the basics and there are suggestions, but we all adopt our own style (not everyone is a NASCAR driver right?).

The point of each of the ideas is to have something that you can use to identify your beliefs and then to challenge them. If they hold up and still work, on to the next. If they are limiting, design an experiment, try it, and observe the results!

Now, back to our conversation about systems around you; and let's stay with Jenny and Mark. Jenny's belief was that she wasn't good with money and that it wasn't ladylike to be concerned with money—a belief that was an unintended consequence of her parents wanting to take care of her and, ironically, reduce her stress. When she challenged her belief and presented her findings to her parents, they were thrilled, and it made them aware that Jenny was also thoughtfully challenging their belief that they were doing their best for her.

So when you design an experiment that challenges a belief you have, be aware that you will likely challenge a belief that depends on yours. You are not responsible *for that* belief, but you *are* responsible for your own beliefs, so stay aware. In this case, Jenny's parents were both impressed and delighted, and a new conversation around money opened up for the family.

And Mark and his trip to Paris? He found out how much the trip cost and, looking at his monthly spending, decided that he didn't have enough time to save all he would need, so he asked his parents if they would pay for the trip. His father, a successful entrepreneur, had always encouraged Mark to take advantage of whatever experiences he could; and he thought the Paris trip would be great. But he realized that it was time to have different money conversations with Mark than they had had, so he made this proposal: He would loan Mark the money for the trip, but Mark needed to pay 10 percent of the trip cost in advance and he needed to apply for the loan. Sounds harsh? His father wanted Mark to experience what applying for a loan could be like and to be able to articulate what this experience would add in his life—was it worth the money? He also wanted Mark to experience paying back a loan on schedule.

So what did Mark do? He weighed his options and figured out a saving schedule that resulted in his saving the entire cost of the trip, and spending money, before the plane took off for Paris.

When you begin to experiment with your own beliefs, you will bump up against the systems those beliefs were formed in. The work, as you go through your experiment, is sorting out the responsibility: Where does your responsibility for change end and the system begin? You will be successful focusing on your belief and change goal, and sometimes, as in Jenny's case, you will change the system belief or, as in Mark's case, the system will give you options to choose.

Remember, you have a brain that allows you to change your beliefs, your behavior, your habits, and your patterns. Some people act as if, "I'm this way, I can't change" and will carry on as if they are animals that, lovable as they are, have no flexibility. You do have that flexibility; whatever your money story is right now, you can change it so that you are able to get where you want with your money.

## SUMMARY

We all have a "money story"; it doesn't have to be true, or consistent, but we tend to act as if it is.

Much of it comes from our family environment, our parents and siblings, and there are influences from our culture, our schools, and our local community.

We have more powerful, flexible brains than other animals, but we don't use their full capacity all the time.

Our brain *rewires* itself, to mean that regular events, such as repeating our money story each time we think about money, makes stronger connections and cuts clearer pathways for certain thoughts.

Which means that we tend to act automatically, like other animals, unless we deliberately stop and think.

You can start unpacking some of your money story, using the exercises and ideas here.

To break out of the habitual pattern of the money story, you may be able simply to do something different.

You may need to work more methodically, using the A, B, C, D, E process.

# Chapter 3

# Setting Your Goals

How do you decide what you're aiming for and where to start planning your finances?

If you read books about being successful in business, particularly the ones that emphasize time management, you'll find they keep talking about doing the important things first, getting your priorities right. That's a good idea, in theory.

And that's the problem, isn't it? You hear about what you *should* be doing, and you think "no s\*\*t Sherlock" and try to put a plan in place and then life gets in the way of your plan!

Honestly, you're going to college; you're smart enough to know you're supposed to do the important stuff first—give us a break. What you need to know is

(a) **how do you select** the most important thing to do for you, at the point you're at, and
(b) **how do you make yourself** do it when you'd rather do something else?

We'll talk about b) later on, but what do you need for a) selecting your priorities?

You need *to be really clear* about what is important to you. That means knowing what you, yourself, absolutely *must* have to get where you want to go and what might be nice but isn't actually vital. You also need to know where you are right now. And once you have those, you can define clear priorities and goals to focus you on what you need to do to get from where you are to where you want to be.

Chapter 1 was about what is important and distinguishing vital from nice but not so important. Chapter 2 was about where you're coming from. And this chapter is about setting *your* priorities.

Because this is about what *you* want, the balance that will get you where *you* want to get. It's not what other people tell you that you ought to want, your "money story" has always made you think you must have, or what an "expert" says you should prioritize. It is tempting to let someone else set your priorities and do the boring budgeting part; because that lets you go off and do things that are more enjoyable. But, in the long run, it is not as satisfying or productive and it doesn't get you where *you* want to go, but where somebody else thinks you *ought* to go. My aim is to help you select your priorities and give you tools to get them done! And who knows? In the process, you might find strengths you didn't know you had!

The next few chapters of the book are about things like living expenses, paying for your social life, insurance, and so on. The relative importance of those elements depends on what *you* want, what is important to *you*. So I can't tell you what you should do first, whether you should sort out your food or your rent or your insurance or your social life, *nor can anybody else*. The priority order will depend on you, your personality, your circumstances, your reason for going to college at all. So you have to work out those priorities for yourself. This is something that most people either don't know to do or can't be bothered to do.

So I aim to help you to work out how to make sure that you do get all the things done, in priority order, so you can get your money to work for you to get you where you want to be. And a big step in doing that is to get your financial goals established.

You'll probably have heard about goal setting. You might have heard it is a good way to increase motivation. In fact, of something like 11 different theories of motivation that you learn in a psychology undergraduate degree, goal setting theory is the only one with really good evidence that it works!

You might even have used goal setting. Perhaps you were told that all goals are supposed to be SMART (typically Specific, Measurable, Achievable, Realistic, Timed). Sadly, although it's well known, it isn't always much help in real life. It misses out too many things that show as key in the research and most important are key in the real world, and one of the ideas behind this book is that the ideas here work in real life, not just in theory.

## WHAT A GOAL MAY NEED

Using the results of many research studies, and a lot of work with people setting and achieving financial goals, let's have a look at what it's useful for *your* goals to contain. I'll give you some examples of how it applies and a way to remember it all if you don't have the book handy, in a while.

### Valuable for Long-Term Happiness

Goals need to fit in with whatever your values are, such as your reason for being at college. You want to be happy in life, so if the goal isn't going to help you end up where you want to be, in something that you enjoy, how will it motivate you? You may not be *certain* how happy you'll be in a new situation, but you can ask yourself questions, such as "do I like this?" or "if I don't like this, will it result in something that I *do* like?" For example, if you realize you like the ocean, but sciences are not a strong suit, will you major in oceanography and work through the academics because you love the ocean or is there another path?

### Specific

If you don't know what you're trying to do, it is tricky to plan to do it. This is the S of the conventional SMART goal. If you want to have *enough* money, that's not a useful goal—how much, really, is *enough* (remember Ed and Judy, our couple who thought they'd be wealthy if they had $50,000 more and that wasn't "enough")? You want to know what that goal is, in dollars and cents, so you know exactly what you're aiming for.

### Exciting

This is another one that SMART doesn't cater to. The difference with this one is that it usually needs to be short term (and will change as you go through different stages in your life), whereas the values are long term and central to your overall makeup. This is where I usually get questions, so if the reason why this is important is obvious to you, skip on, but if not, here's why.

Happiness, having a life you really enjoy, is a lot more than brief pleasure. Your happiness over your life will depend on years of different things: working at a job you like, meeting people, having experiences, helping others. You're going to spend four (or maybe more) years at college, and that's a fairly long time (particularly in terms of your age now) and it's intended to be of value to you in terms of happiness for forty years or more. Now does the thought of being happy at 50 float your boat? It did nothing for me. When I was 18, I thought 25 was old; I couldn't even imagine being as old as my parents. That's where lots of conventional financial planning is useless. People will tell you to contribute to a 401K because you need to plan ahead, the earlier you start the better, you'll be glad when you're 50 that you started saving at 20, and so on. That makes sense. It's also really boring and does nothing to get you going!

You're smart. You know that you *should* save for the future and that investing in a pension is a *good* idea. And you know that there is no way you're going to do it, because there are loads of things that, right now, are more exciting and that you need and want your money for. Human beings didn't evolve to plan 40 years ahead (the life expectancy of humans, 20,000 plus years ago, was probably less than 40 anyway). We evolved to think about what we'd eat today and sometimes maybe next week. Our brains haven't changed that much. That's one reason we have an obesity epidemic: Food is easy to get, ready to eat almost any time and we tend to eat when we take breaks from our sedentary (boring?) job—we don't have to work at getting it and burn off energy hunting or preparing it.

We don't get excited about long-term goals, although those are the ones we really want to get to, because they are "way out there." But if you have a long-term goal and a series of exciting short-term goals that add up to your long-term goal, you are likely to get to your long-term goal before you know it. You are more likely to do well in a marathon if you've actually done some training to build up stamina in the six months before, aren't you? You want something that's going to get you to do something *now*.

In money terms, that might be a short-term goal of making payments for a car, which is a motivator right now and will get you out of bed at six on a cold, dark morning to do a part-time job before lectures. If you think only in terms of the long-term value of being an architect, a CPA, or whatever in 10 years' time, some mornings you're going to hit the snooze button and go back to sleep. It just won't motivate you like the thought of missing a payment and having the car taken away. By the same token, in the long run, the car isn't going to give you as much value and happiness as the career you really enjoy and find value in.

So you probably need both long-term and short-term goals.

### Aligned

And you want your longer term values-based goal and shorter term, exciting goal pulling in the same direction. Otherwise you'll get all excited about getting further and further from your long-term goal and values!

### Timed

It's often handy if your goal has a timescale, which is one of the *must-haves* in SMART. However, the point is to get action, so a time set for a short-term goal is very likely to be important. Having a "time limit" on a life value and a long-term goal might just make you stressed over it. If you've got the shorter term goal right, it will be motivating and exciting and will get you moving in the right direction toward your longer term goal anyway. Have you ever noticed how much you get done right before you are leaving on a trip? This is the same idea ... plan several trips!

### Action Based

It needs to include something that you can actually *do*—not a wish list. Your value in life (like, "create beautiful buildings") might be abstract, but the goal needs to contain action steps that you can take, not vague things like, "each day try to be a better person." Again, not something that SMART bothers about, which is why so many "goals" are actually vague dreams that never get achieved.

### Controllable

You want to be able to do it with your own actions. This is something else that SMART misses out. But it's important. Some things in life you can control; some you can't. For example, if you play tennis, you might decide you want to beat Nadal on clay. But you can't control him, so however good you are on the day, he might be better. What you can control is what you do. So you can, for example, practice your serve so that your first serve percentage is 85, rather than the pro-circuit average of about 71 percent. You still might not win, but you make it harder for him to break your serve, and you are working on something you control, not something that you don't.

As an example from investing, you will not be able to control fund performance, so you might have a problem with "my goal is to have a fund worth X," but you can control how much you put into the fund, what expenses you have to pay, and so on.

### Adaptable

If the fund performance, for example, is much better or worse than you anticipated, do you have a *fallback* position or a plan b? Ideally, your goal can be adapted easily to changing circumstances.

### Measurable

You want to know where you are, the M of the SMART goal. It probably means having particular outcomes, not just processes. With investments, "make some investments" is a process, but "put X amount into an index tracking fund each month" could be an outcome you can measure success with.

### Planned

You want to know what you have to do, to have an action plan. That way, you can get on and do things, not get stuck wondering how best to achieve your goal. Again, this is one that SMART simply doesn't cover, but many people have dreams they don't reach because the dreams remained just dreams and never actually became plans—the money classic being, "if I have some money at the end of the month, I'll save it." So the plan might be to put money away at the start of the month, so it's a definite plan not a wish—it doesn't have an *if*. Once you've put the money away, you probably won't have any trouble spending what is left, but that way you've got the money saved that month and every month following and head toward the goal.

### Little Steps

Small scale (both in resources and time), simple steps that are properly organized get you to goals. Grand ideals involving millions of dollars and decades of time don't, unless you're very lucky, and the point is to reach the goals and remove the need for luck. It's a bit like the difference between long-term goals (values based) and short-term ones. So you usually need to break big goals down into smaller steps that you can take action on now and build them up to achieve the big goals in due course.

### Resourced

This is often a difficult one. You may not know what resources you need until you know the goal, and you don't know what you can realistically plan for until you know what relevant resources you have. You might also not know what resources are relevant (such as not knowing about rental costs of property, what insurance is available, how you can economize on spending, and so on).

The essential feature about resources for goals is that there are two opposing forces involved. There's good evidence that a goal that is challenging, that stretches you, is more motivating. If it's too easy, there's no fun. It's similar to the concept of "flow," introduced by Mihaly Csikszentmihalyi. If your ability is high and the challenge low, you become bored easily. That applies with mundane jobs, with an opponent that you can beat easily, a puzzle that is too simple, or a novice slope if you're a black run skier. If you have an easy goal, for which you've got more than enough resources in terms of money, time, ability, and so on, it won't motivate you. If you've already been promised a car for your GPA so far, whatever you do, you're going to get the car. It's not a good goal as it is not going to motivate you to study at all.

On the other hand, if the challenge is high and your ability low, you become stressed. Imagine a new project you don't feel you can handle, a challenge match against the person who always beats you, an insoluble puzzle, or a terrifying slope for you as a novice skier. With financial resources, for example, your goal may be to save an amount that some expert has deemed "reasonable" each month, and your challenge is that it is more than you have coming in before you make allowance for all your living costs. The challenge is so great that it terrifies you, your automatic "fight or flight" response kicks in, and you stop thinking consciously.

What you want is something where the challenge and the resources match, which is the point of "flow." Think of it as taking on an opponent that you have to play at your best to beat, the puzzle that most people can't tackle but you know you can if you're at your best, or the black ski run that you fly down. If you've ever experienced that (and I know you have, several times), you'll know how time seems to stand still, you're totally focused, you perform at your best, you get terrific satisfaction, and you feel on top of the world.

So you want something like that with your goals and your resources. You don't want it too easy, because that's no fun and it's not motivating. You don't want it too hard because that's scary and not motivating. You want the "Goldilocks point," where it's not too hard, not too soft, but just right to push you to your best work and motivate you, but not intimidate you.

You might want some professional help with some of the issues around resources, but I'll give you some examples that you can adapt in this chapter, and in the rest of the book, there will be lots of ideas for questions to ask about different aspects so that you can work out what resources you need.

## Positively Worded

Your mind doesn't work well with negatives. For example, if I say, "don't think of elephants," what do you think of? Elephants, of course! In order for you to avoid thinking of something (whether it's "don't eat too much," "don't buy an expensive designer coffee every day," or something else), your brain is focused on the forbidden thing so that you can avoid it—you are ready to defend yourself from whatever threat you are aware of! This is one reason, among many others, that diets fail. People think about foods they can't have while they are "dieting" instead of designing an eating plan they will try out for, say, a month and assessing how they feel at the end of that time. So their attention is on the food they mustn't eat and because that food is front and center, they eat it!

There's been a lot of research on this and some of the most striking is in sports coaching. For examples, elite golfers focus on sinking putts, not on missing them and tennis players focus on where they want to hit their service, not where they don't want it to go. You will be more likely to reach a goal that is positive ("I'll have enough money to pay for a social life as well as expenses") than one that is negative ("I won't run out of money and be unable to pay my bills or have a social life")—your brain is not engaging its "fight or flight" tendency! That positive wording, of course, is the final step in defining your goals—after you are sure that it aligns with your values and you've figured out exactly (or as closely as you can) how much *enough* is!

## Noted Down

Again there's a lot said about this (including studies at Yale and Harvard that are widely quoted but that research indicates never took place)! A written goal is probably more likely to be achieved, but any improvement in completion seems to come from reviewing the goal and it being available—carried with you or taped to your bathroom mirror so you see it every time you brush your teeth, so increasing your motivation because of the reminder of the time and energy it took to define it. It might also motivate you because of the embarrassment of sharing it with other people or having said you'll do it, and then not doing it. That brings us to another feature of motivation.

There's research by Professor Higgins at Columbia about "Regulatory Focus." Put simply, people can use one of two reference points to judge their behavior (which might be to get up and do the job, or turn over and go back to sleep). One reference point is our private self, our thoughts, feelings, and attitudes. That will usually mean comparing actual events to our own ideal, our own model of what we'd like. The other reference point is our public self, the way others see us, our social image. That will usually mean that we compare actual events to what we feel ought to be done, to a model of what we see as social expectations.

Both types of people will respond better to positively worded goals. But they are likely to differ in exactly why the goals motivate them. Taking a golfing example, a golfer who references the private self ("promotion focus") will be motivated by the positive consequences of holing the putt. One who references the public self ("prevention focus") will be motivated by avoiding the consequences of missing the putt. They both work to hole it, and they both focus on holing it and not on missing it, but the reason they do it is based on different motivations. So a promotion-focused person will probably relate to the goal because of the time and energy she or he put in, the internal effort. The prevention-focused person will probably relate to the goal because it would be embarrassing to fail relative to the public expectation he or she has set up.

It's worth saying that these different approaches are a bit like having blue or brown eyes; they are the way we are, they're not really something we can change, and there isn't a "right way" to be. But as with knowing about what you want a goal to do, it's useful to know why it works for you because if you understand yourself and your motives better, you can make sure that your goals are set to give you the best possible chance to achieve them.

## A Summary of What Goals Need

That probably sounds like a lot of things to remember. But you can sit down and plan this; you don't have to carry it all in your head—so it's an "open book" exam. You might not need all of the points, but if you've got a reminder of them, it gives you the best chance to achieve your goals.

If you want to remember all the points for yourself, so that you can run a check on your goals in your head, the best way is to make up your own mnemonic, a song, a picture, and so on. Human memory is constructive—it loves a story—and if you build it, you'll remember it. If somebody else tells you how to remember it, you'll probably forget it. However, the mnemonic I use is


## Cheap Smart Plan

When I'm setting a goal with a client (or for myself—this is the way I set my own goals), I run through that in my head and check that those things that it makes sense to define and clarify have been defined and clarified.

The letters stand for these elements of your goal:

Controllable (you control it; you're not at somebody else's mercy as to whether you reach it or not)

Happy (in the long term, it will make you happy)

Exciting (in the short term, it will get you out of bed)

Aligned (the long and the short term are in the same direction)

Positively worded (it aims at a good outcome, rather than starting out to avoid something unpleasant)

Specific (you know what it is and will know when you've reached it)

Measurable (you know how far you've come and how far you have to go by outcomes)

Adaptable (if things go better or worse than expected, there is somewhere to go with the goal)

Resourced (it is achievable from where you are, but it might be a stretch)

Timed (you know when things, particularly actions, are expected to happen)

Planned (it is set out as a plan, not a vague wish that something would happen)

Little steps (this fits with measurement of progress; it doesn't leave yawning gaps)

Action based (it is about doing things, not waiting for chance)

Noted (it is recorded somewhere, shown to people as a potential source of embarrassment if not done, or a reminder of your own commitment)

## Examples

I said I'd give you an example to show how this works. It deals with what are regarded as quite complex financial issues, but the finances are pretty simple—it is the people who are complicated!

You remember **Terri** wants to be an architect. She knows clearly what she is after and she's identified the three courses that she really wants, which will be the best for her development. All of them involve her moving away from home, which creates a list of "needs" and "wants": somewhere to live (presumably for money), living expenses (food, transportation, clothing, perhaps a cell phone), some money for social events (she won't have her home town connections to meet up with). So that all need to be sorted out.

But the priority for her is getting some work experience. Terri knows that what often sets the successful job seeker (qualified or not) from the unsuccessful is having some experience. That's not just because some-body who has at least some experience is more valuable; it's because they are seen to be more "go-getting" and more resourceful. So she wants to get a vacation job that has at least some connection to architecture. She's going to have to work in the summer vacation anyway because her family doesn't have the money to have the whole summer as holiday. She has decided that she will focus on entry-level office work rather than other hourly options (serving coffee, waitressing, or flipping burgers) because it is more in line with the type of atmosphere she wants to work toward as an architect.

So Terri has her long-term goal (architect) and her short-term goal (experience). She'll work with real architects and have some insight into how they work, what really happens with a project, how an office runs, what the "unwritten rules" are. So when she comes to a placement year or her first job after qualifying, she's got an edge.

And her short-term goal (experience) is aligned with her long-term goal. She can start working on that, which will give her an idea of what sort of vacation income she can make to provide for living expenses during term time.

How does it fit with what we know about goal setting?

It's exciting, linked to her values, and controllable; it's specific; and it ticks all the boxes except that she needs a plan for what she's going to do, the actions she's going to take, and some measures and timescales for the "little steps."

So she needs to break down the "get a job" idea into some steps.

If you're applying for a job (and pretty well everybody does, at some point), there are three basic approaches. One is to network, to make and ask friends as well as relatives, teachers, career tutors, and so on for leads. Another is what I call the "sniper" approach; you research the organization, find out who to contact, and target specific people and organizations. The third is what I call the "scatter gun" approach; you send out résumés to everybody who might possibly offer you a role.

You can obviously mix those together, depending on your situation. Networking depends on the contacts you've got, or can create. It might get you something; it's certainly worth asking at least for some contact details if you want to go for the targeted approach, and for potential employers if you want to approach a lot of organizations. The sniper approach requires research, which you may be able to do via network contacts. Or you may need to look up the details of companies, who to contact, what sort of qualities they want, via business libraries, on the Internet, and so on. The scatter gun approach is the easiest one to use in isolation; you don't really need to network or research, although your network might provide some organizations to whom you can send a résumé.

The scatter gun approach therefore sounds a lot easier. It used to mean typing or hand writing (seriously!) dozens of letters and résumés, mailing them off, keeping lists of who you'd mailed to in a book. Now you can just prepare a single electronic résumé and email it to everybody. So it used to be that all three methods involved quite a lot of work, and then the scatter gun approach got much simpler relative to the others. Because humans are "cognitively economical" (remember, our brains use lots of fuel, so we don't think too hard unless we have to), most people mailed off hundreds of electronic résumés, and hiring managers got swamped.

So they also used technology to make their job easier, by developing résumé readers with auto response mail systems, candidate tracking systems, automated shortlist compilers based on key word searches, third-party Internet sites with filters, and plenty of other ways to simplify the task of wading through the thousands of résumés and applications they might receive for a job vacancy.

So you've still got the basic choices. You can network as a personal contact is useful; people buy people not résumés. You can do your research and try to target what they want and demonstrate how you can provide it. And you can apply broadly and hope that your résumé is going to trip the key words at one of the organizations and get you on the shortlist.

Terri decided to do a mixture of approaches. She would do other things as well, but first she prepared three or four versions of her résumé, which each emphasizes different combinations of skills that she thought might interest an employer, with different key words (that she's researched) that seem to be in favor with recruiters. She e-mailed these in response to job advertisements and kept notes of any that produced positive responses. If she got a job that way, fine. If not, it could give her some clues as to what aspects, and what words, were likely to get her to the next stage.

While she was waiting for responses, she used her network and worked on some target organizations.

Think of that in terms of goals. All these variables are controllable; Terri is the one in charge and she can get up early, research late, do whatever she wants. She can plan her steps. She can get on the Internet and look for architect businesses local to her home (to start with). She can look at the size of the organizations, what work they specialize in, what clients they have, whether they have intern programs, offer placements, and so on. Terri can call and find out who would make hiring decisions and get their contact details. She can decide how broadly to spread the net away from architects to general businesses if she wants to apply more of a scatter gun approach.

As measures of progress, Terri can decide on a certain number of contacts that she'll be ready to write to or e-mail each week. If it proves hard to get the right details, she'll have to put more work in; if she gets some good leads from her contacts, she'll have it easier so it's adaptable. Whatever happens, she'll know whether she's on course, and she'll have some ways to measure how she's doing. But in tailoring her résumé and approach, whether it's broad mailing round or specifically targeted, she's up against another common problem for high-school and college graduates. She doesn't seem to have much to offer, having no experience or qualifications yet.

This is relevant to any job you might apply for. It might seem as if it has nothing to do with planning your money, but it's very relevant. In first jobs one of the greatest assets you have is enthusiasm. You're not cynical and worn down by years of doing something you don't really like to make a buck, like 60 percent of the workforce (hard to believe, right?). You are (if you've taken to heart the first chapter) really excited by what you're studying. If you apply that excitement to a job application (that's going to enable you to get experience, or at least to earn the money to study the subject you want), you're going to come over as being enthusiastic, ready to work hard, and learn fast.

When we looked at it for real, Terri had several things to offer, and you'll find that if you apply the same thought and research, you have too. We found Terri had:

*Drawing and card modeling skills.* This was part of what interested her in architecture in the first place, what made it something she really wanted to do—she is good at practical drawing and at building models. That's a skill many people don't have, it can be very useful to architect firms, and Terri made sure she's got some examples of how she can use that natural talent to help with typical architecture issues.

*She scores well on tests of ability to visualize things in 3D*, the sort of test where you have to imagine what flat shapes look like "folded up." That means she's got skills useful to an architect such as turning 2-D blueprints into a 3-D model in her head. Again, it's an inherent skill; something that she finds "flow" in using and she's made sure she's got some test results to show any potential employers.

*Computer-Aided Design (CAD) skills.* Terri's grown up with the Internet, with phone apps, Facebook, Twitter, and so on. Experienced architects (like many professionals) are mostly older; many grew up and got their experience in a different environment. They may not have good keyboard skills and certainly aren't automatically comfortable with technology. Because Terri's interested, she'd learned about CAD, tried out some of the common software packages (through her high-school resources), and, if she gets an interview, can demonstrate what she can do (because she's researched and prepared some simple but impressive looking examples).

*She's organized and can do general administration.* That's not an exceptional skill. But there are a lot of people who can't be trusted to file documents accurately, keep a general diary up to date, book meetings and journeys without forgetting details, and follow up when they haven't heard back or confirm when they have. Terri's made sure that when she's done things like that (for societies and clubs at high school and outside) she has kept some endorsements from responsible people and has got notes of examples that she can give in interviews. And she demonstrates these skills in *real time* during the job search process: by following up on her leads, by sending *thank you* notes after interviews, and by reviewing and "tweaking" her plan. You may think these are just manners or maybe you think they are too time consuming, but they are real skills that can show a potential employer what kind of hire you will be. If you haven't used these skills, they are good to experiment with now—like your money habits they will become part of the way you succeed!

*And she's got real enthusiasm.* Particularly in offices with low turnover of staff, a young, energetic person who cares about the job (however menial) and who really wants to learn can make a huge difference.

So Terri is in a position to set out that goal, in as much detail as is useful to her. She can plan her research to get the background on potential employers and to find key words and useful variants on her résumé. She can get contact details and tailor her résumé to make it appealing to each contact. She can think about how to demonstrate what she's got to offer an employer at an interview and work on some good examples. She can set herself measures of progress (numbers of contacts, details of organizations, application letters, and so on) and she can set herself timescales to get things done (so many per week, for example). If family or friends come up with a good lead, she can adapt to that (call and check what they want, tailor her résumé, prepare for interview). If she's not getting much response, she can try different wordings or variants of skills (or persist, a lot of the time you just have to keep going—which is why it's important to be motivated).

You may not want to be an architect, so the ideas about 3D don't apply to you. But you know what your talents are (e.g., if you did the VIA), and you can do the same sort of research, tailoring of your résumé, and so on. But you need to work out your timescales, your measures of progress, your positive goal ("getting job experience and earning some money"), the action plan that puts you in control (not, "wait for Uncle Bob to find me something"), and so on.

I said in the last chapter that we'd look at how Mark set up his goals. I gave you the result, how his father suggested loaning Mark the money if Mark put up 10 percent of the trip cost and applied for a loan, how Mark built a new relationship with his father in the process, and how he actually took responsibility and set up a savings schedule to save the whole cost himself.

What I didn't say was how he did that.

Mark realized two things when his father suggested the loan and the conditions. The first was that he really wanted to go to Paris because of his interest in new experiences and people. He also realized that he really valued his independence, and being in debt to his father for 90 percent of the cost of the trip felt to him like he was gaining experience but giving away his independence. So, he looked again at his spending and thought about how he could shift his spending for the six months he had before the trip. He found that his budget was 25 percent "needs" (housing, food, transport) and 75 percent "wants" (a very big cable bill, a gym membership he never used, dinners out with friends that cost way more than he needed to spend to keep in contact), and he made short-term shifts to reach his trip goal. The shift in the relationship with his father came when he shared the plan with him: Mark felt as if he was speaking to his father as a peer or business partner because he had worked out a plan and was asking for input.

## SUMMARY

The purpose of a goal is to motivate you to do something—if it doesn't do that, it isn't working.

One thing it can do is help you to focus on the priorities, the things you need to do first.

You can use the "Cheap Smart Plan" mnemonic to remember what elements of a goal to check on, but it's a good idea to make up your own way to remember it, or to refer to the book, to make sure you've got all the elements you need.

You can use the stories of Terri and Mark as examples of how you can set about setting your goals for finances.

Chapter 4

# Where Should You Live? At Home? On Campus? Off Campus?

It's not always the greatest expense, either at college or in life, but housing tends to produce the strongest emotions. People in many cultures take a lot of notice of property—hence the number of magazines, TV programs, column inches, and so on dedicated to celebrity homes.

That means it's even more important than normal to have a clear head when making housing decisions, or it can cause you a lot of pain as well as cost you a lot of money!

The aim of this chapter (and the next few) is slightly different from the first three. Those were entirely about you, where you are, and where you want to be. It really didn't matter what anybody else thought; you were the entire focus. Here, it's still about you, but it's looking for the methods to get you where you want to go from where you are. So you need to be able to find the facts you need to slot into your plans and your goals.

That means that there are still questions for you to ask yourself, for example about how much you're willing to trade or give up for something you want and what aspects of a situation are most important to you. But now there will be more questions for you to ask other people. Those questions are going to allow you to get the facts so that you can build *your* plans, to get to *your* goals and values.

When you look at housing options for college, there are three broad categories: *family home, college dorms,* and living *off campus.* They've all got advantages and disadvantages, which you may see differently than "the experts," so this still starts—and ends—with *you.*

First you need to ask yourself questions, and I'll get to specifics in a minute. You also need to ask other people questions and do research about what you are required to do—perhaps live in dorms for the freshman year—and you need to get the facts about the costs of different options (like having a room to yourself) so that you know what is possible. You may need to set out an "ideal" situation to suit yourself, then adapt it for what is possible and affordable, and then adjust your plan to fit the resources you have. You're looking for the "Goldilocks point," where you get the deal that you want, that may be a stretch of your money (or your tolerance of other people!), but that works for you. You don't want to be dictated to by what "most people" like. You also don't want something that suits you fine as far as housing goes but bankrupts you in the first semester! It sounds complicated, but stick with me—this is a tool you will use often when you are making decisions about your money.

I'll look at each of those categories in turn, and give you some things to consider and questions to ask yourself and other people, to get to where you can make a plan that works for you.

## LIVING AT THE FAMILY HOME

This option is realistically only available if you're going to college near home. The family home can obviously be cheaper, which gives you more scope to use your budget on other things, but it is not necessarily the best option. You might actually want to pay rent to your parents and make a contribution to the household even if your parents don't insist on it. That's connected to another aspect, responsibility. There's a balance between taking on the responsibility of being an adult (being accountable for your actions, paying your own way, making your own decisions, and taking the consequences whatever they are) and being a full-time student. As a student, your full-time "job" is to learn your subject and hopefully get good grades; it's not to earn a full-time working wage and be a provider.

You may decide to establish that you are taking steps into adulthood and responsibility when you go to college. Perhaps you want to demonstrate that you are not so dependent on your parents, make more decisions, be more accountable, have more financial responsibility. That comes automatically if you live away from home. If you live at home, you can take the same steps and show you are taking them by arranging to pay your parents what you would need to pay a landlord or the college if you were living away—or at least agree on a portion of what the rent would be, if you can't afford the entire amount.

Along with that responsibility also goes some element of freedom. However understanding your parents are, they are still your parents, and it's often very hard for them to let go and allow you to make what they see as your own "mistakes" (which you see as living your own life) without at least *wanting* to interfere. That might be about friends, over-night guests, drinking habits, working hours—but whatever it is, it's ulti-mately their home and their rules (in most cases, anyway), and there are limits to how far you can, or would want to, push the boundaries.

That gives you some things to think about for yourself. If you are looking at a college near home, ask yourself about how much freedom and respon-sibility you would like (they go together!) and how much that costs.

You might do as Mark did in the last chapter and make an arrangement with your parents. You could have a conversation and develop an agree-ment about living at the house while you are in school. This agreement would cover rent as well as house rules, which may include use of facilities (kitchen and laundry), guest privileges (when and where and how often they are allowed), parties—well, you get the idea. Anything you would negotiate with a landlord, you can negotiate with your parents—including the penal-ties for transgression on either side of the agreement. In this you need to decide how much you are prepared to accept their rules and prioritize their judgments ahead of your own, in return for being able to have more discre-tionary money than you would if living independently.

Only you can answer those questions, but it might help you to think about what your alternatives and potential trade-offs are to consider—and investigate—the other options than living at home.

## LIVING IN THE COLLEGE DORM

You've got some certainty here. There will be dorms, there might be fraternity or sorority houses as well—but there will be somewhere to stay! Other than that, you really need to do your research in terms of what it costs, what you get for your money, what the rules are, and also what you want and how the various options work for you. Even if the policy of the college is to assign first-year students to dorms and assign room-mates, there are usually options to consider (e.g., a double room, a suite, a coed dorm, a dorm with all freshmen or mixed upper classmen and freshmen).

One aspect you need to think about is that this is going to be your home for a period, the first year at least. The campus residence hall may be the first time you've lived away from home for an extended period, so it's helpful to consider it carefully, possibly thinking about it from different angles, in different moods, and so on. It's easy, when you're feeling optimistic, to get carried away with how great it will be to be free, to have no parents waiting up for you, and to feel totally confident and in control; however in that mood there is a danger that you could commit yourself beyond what you can cope with. It's also easy, when you feel a bit down, to imagine lousy conditions, horrible roommates, and total isolation and, scare yourself out of an opportunity.

It is often worth using techniques like mindfulness described in Chapter 1, to make sure you're able to get a clear view of the pros and cons of a situation.

It is also helpful if you have a clear idea of where you want to go, to narrow down your choices. That means knowing why you're there at all, what courses you want to follow, what you want to get out of the experience, and the other points linked to your values, as in Chapter 1. That might sound strange. You'd think it would be better to be able to go to any college so you'd have more choice, more options of housing (and everything else). But it's another oddity of the human mind. If we have more choice, we find it harder to make a decision. We're also likely to regret the choice we made more and be less enthusiastic about sticking with it if it turns out to be more difficult than we thought. (If you want to look it up, there's a classic paper about it, http://psy2.ucsd.edu /~nchristenfeld/DoG_Readings_files/Class%209%20-%20Iyengar% 202000.pdf, or you can just search for "jam experiment" [seriously] and you'll find lots of discussion and some fun examples.)

The key point is that if you've defined what you want clearly enough, you've got a smaller set of options, a more limited range of colleges that offer the courses you want so you've got a more solid base for your decisions. That means you're less likely to regret your choices and you're odds on to pursue your values with real enthusiasm.

There are likely to be some constraints on your choices at a given college. Some require you to live in dorms in your freshman year and sometimes your sophomore year as well—some don't. You may be used to your own room at home; at college you may be sharing your dorm room with at least one other person, and maybe more. Some campus dorms have private bathrooms. In other cases, you'll be sharing them with the entire floor. The amenities may or may not include air conditioning, microwaves, and refrigerators, and those (and your own room, or bathroom) may be standard, may be extras (for which you pay extra), or may not be available.

See what I mean? If you know which college (or a limited number of colleges) you really want, it's actually easier to choose. If you have the choice of hundreds of colleges, each with hundreds of options, it's hard to keep all the details straight—and it becomes easy to let the choices be made by other people, instead of you deciding what is important for you. For example, at some colleges, freshmen are required to live in the dorms but may move off campus as upperclassmen. At others, nearly all students stay in the dormitories.

You might have noticed those points were worded slightly differently—you might be required to do something, but in another place it's what *nearly all people* do. You're not *nearly all people*; you're *you*. Make sure you know what choices are requirements for where you want to go, and which ones you can make for yourself. It might be more expensive, it might be less convenient, or there might be all sorts of difficulties with the choice you want to make. But if something like being off campus (or on)—your own room, the facilities you have—or some other aspects are really important to you, you may be able to make conscious decisions to fund them, live with any problems, and have the setup that works for you.

There are a lot of variables, even if you have many external requirements limiting your options, and you will improve your information gathering if you actually visit and get the details. If you can't visit in person, many colleges offer virtual college tours online, allowing you to view photos and maps of the campus or even take a peek inside a residence hall. Just keep in mind that those photos are chosen by the university to show off the best and most attractive areas of campus. So you probably want to find out another way to get details aside from the "official" version.

For a more balanced view you can search for the online edition of the student newspaper for photos and information about current events on campus. The college may also have a school-sponsored blog, or you can search for blogs created by current students.

Remember, whatever you're doing, to think about what it is like in terms of what you want. If you come from a major urban area, perhaps you want to be in a small, close-knit community for a change. Perhaps if it didn't have the social setup you're used to, it would be too quiet and make you uncomfortable. Only you know the answer to those sorts of questions, and you'll only find out by getting the information on the college, in whatever way you can.

Ideally, you'll visit the colleges that you may be going to (it's time and money, but it's going to be four years of your life and it's worth getting what you want). You can see the buildings, student housing, and other facilities, as well as get an idea of the campus size, the way it's set out, and the *feel* of the place. You will also learn how easy—or difficult—it is to get transportation to and from school for future reference (holidays, graduation!).

If you can, it's useful to see whether you can sample the campus while school is in progress. Some colleges sponsor a program for potential students to stay overnight in a dorm. The college may pair you with a current student, and you can learn firsthand about having roommates and sharing a bathroom! You'll have more time to see the campus, and your temporary roomie could take you to sample the cafeteria, show you the surrounding community, and fill you in on the best nearby eateries, bookstores, and so on. Also, the more time you spend there, the more chance you have to ask other students about life on that campus.

If you are going (even for a few hours), it's a good idea to call the college in advance to schedule a tour. A guided tour will give you a good overview of the campus. It will also provide you with an opportunity to meet students at the school, so it's another chance to get some "unofficial" information. Leave enough time during your campus visit to check out areas you're interested in (with or without a roomie, guide, or other friend you've met on the day). A few examples: you might want to visit the student union or another busy area and watch the students and see how the social atmosphere seems. If you like to work out, take a look at the gym and sports facilities. If you like to read, check out the campus library. And if you have time, try out the cafeteria(s); if you're going to eat there during your time, you want food that fits your tastes as well as your budget.

If you visit on a weekday during the school year, you might even be able to sit in on a class (or three). I'd suggest taking notes and pictures; you're probably going to visit more than one college and it could become difficult to remember which campus had the great gym and/or the pokey library.

There are a lot of different things you could ask, so it's not an exhaustive list, but here are some suggestions. A note: no matter who is paying for your education and housing, the following questions are important for you to consider. As I've said a few times, this is your experience, and you can learn a lot about decision making as you go through this process, which you will use over and over again in different situations.

### Official questions on housing

- Can students choose which dorm they live in? Is there a choice of single gender or coed?
- What amenities (air conditioning, refrigerator, bathroom, and so on) do the rooms have? Are there extra costs for "upgrades?" Generally, a single room with air conditioning and a private bathroom will cost more than a room for four with bunk beds, but ask!
- Are the charges the same? (Some colleges charge freshmen more for housing than they do for returning students.)
- How many roommates are assigned to a dorm room? Does the number vary?
- How are roommates chosen? Do you get any input?
- Do all students live on campus? Do only freshmen?
- What types of security measures are in place at the dorms?
- How easy is it to get from the dorms to the classrooms?

Speaking of classrooms, you may already have found these points out but consider asking these questions:

### Official questions on classes

- How easy/difficult is it to enroll in the courses you want?
- How many students are there in the courses you want?
- What is the faculty-student ratio (generally, and particularly for your courses)?
- In theory, how many contact/teaching hours do you spend in classes, seminars, workshops, and so on, and how many hours are you expected to study?
- What contact is possible with your professors, and what sort of office hours do they have?

It's probably another new experience for you; colleges are structured differently to high school. College professors can have hundreds of students in a lecture or seminar, so it can be difficult to get time with them. You probably don't want the experience of a friend of mine who, until he started his PhD, managed to have about four conversations with his assigned tutor, each of them lasting as long as it took to walk (very rapidly) from the lecture hall to the professor's next destination! So it's useful to find out how much you can access your professors—not only can they be a great source of advice and help with issues (academic and nonacademic) but also of referrals when you leave and even as mentors in the future.

There are some other questions that are useful to ask. They're not strictly about housing or even academic activities, but they affect your experience of college life. So they may be aspects that will help you decide exactly where you want to go, if other considerations are equal.

You can ask the questions of the college establishment, look up the details in magazines or the website—but often the best sources of information are existing students.

- How easy is it to get around—for example, between dorms, classrooms, library, sources of part-time job, stores for groceries and other items?
- Can students bring a car to campus?
- Does the college have a campus shuttle service or other system for getting around? How practical is it? Does it run late night?
- Are there fraternities and sororities? How active are they? What proportion of students get involved? Are they basically just social (nothing wrong with that!) or do they have opportunities for volunteering and perhaps leadership (always handy for your résumé)? Do they provide accommodation?
- What types of clubs are on offer? Are there social activities, and do they have career clubs (or something similar) to aid with your progress, job finding after graduation, and so on?
- Does the college have intramural sports?
- What events (speakers, movies, concerts, and so on) does the college host?
- Are on-campus jobs available?

And some other points are really about impressions, so they won't really have an official answer. You might have impressions yourself: you may have sampled the food, you might have felt the atmosphere, you may have noted what styles of clothing the students wear; all of these will give you a feeling for whether you'll fit in. But strangely, we're often not very good at judging what we'll like; one of the best ways to work out whether you'll enjoy something is to ask people who have just done it (hence the success of TripAdvisor). So if you get the chance, you might ask your guide and other new friends on campus:

- How do you like the cafeteria food? How many cafeterias does the college have? Do they all offer the same food? Are there good (and economical) options for eating out or buying groceries to cook yourself? (We'll look at this more when we talk about regular expenses.)
- Do you feel safe on campus? How about off campus? If this seems to be (or you feel) a concern, look for well-lit sidewalks and roads and check cell phone reception.
- What is student life like on the weekends? Weeknights?

- Does the community where the school is located welcome students?
- What do you like best about this college? And what do you like least?

These are all features that might matter to you, and you can see why I don't hold with the idea of "set your budget" before you know what you want. If you feel that you can't possibly stand to share a room or bathroom—and that is the only option at the college—you either have to work out how to stand it or need to find another college that has the courses that you want and where you can have your own room. But—and this is where it hits the budget—you may have to pay extra to have your own room, even if that is an option somewhere. Doing that means that you don't have as much money for something else.

You might want to prioritize food, safety, privacy, access to learning, or a multitude of other things. I can't tell you what you *ought* to prioritize and budget for, and *neither can anybody else.*

So you need the information in order to decide where your budget goes and what resources (remember from goal setting) you have for the different aspects of your life at college.

I will give you one piece of definite advice, though. If people tell you how much money you *ought* to spend on things, or anything like "sharing a room will knock the rough edges off you," that is their opinion and has nothing to do with you, your feelings, and your values; ignore them! Be polite about it, tell them their opinion is informative, and thank them for it; then ignore it and work out what *you* want. It's *your* life and *your* money.

## LIVING OFF CAMPUS

This is something many students relish: renting a place with three or four friends—or at least having somewhere off campus where they can have more freedom and be away from the supervision of both parents and faculty.

Like anything else, you have to decide what works for you and weigh your priorities. Housing off campus typically doesn't have the level of rules regarding alcohol, tobacco, and visitors that students in dorms—or living at home—may face. You may prefer the freedom and extra space provided by your own apartment and be fine with being away from the center of things and having to take more responsibility for yourself. By contrast, you might be more comfortable with less responsibility for bills and chores, generally fewer worries, and the ready-made social scene provided by the dorm environment.

To check out the situation on living off campus at a college, you can ask the college and any guide or friends you've made on a visit. Ask what the rules are about starting in dorms and so on. Find out where the majority of students off campus live and how they live. Are they close to the campus? Is it a safe area? What are the average costs they pay and what sort of facilities do they have? Averages aren't always useful, but might give you a guide to see if you're being realistic in your expectations.

If this looks promising, look in the classified section of the school or city newspaper and visit local rental agencies. And don't be scared to ask for help. Friends and campus offices can assist you and will probably be delighted to do so.

It's worth thinking about the options when you're researching. So decide if you will live off campus alone in your new apartment or with roommates. If you will have roommates, how many? This will determine the number of bedrooms your apartment should have. You might ideally want to have your own place, but when you look at the finances, it isn't feasible. So you have to decide on what balance suits you.

You might, depending on your situation and that of your parents, be able to get them to help you with rents but—as with Mark's situation described in the last chapter—you need to discuss this with them and balance up the degree of autonomy you want compared to the extra facilities, privacy, and so on that you can get with their help if, that is, they are in a position to help you. It may be possible, again depending on them, on the college, and on your powers of persuasion, for them to buy an investment property. We'll look at the outline of that later, but it does take some negotiation and probably a lot of work on your part to make it work effectively.

If you get to the point of serious consideration, where you're going to visit potential apartments, it's a good idea first to scope out what you think you want, whether it's for yourself alone or with potential roommates. If possible, try to have an idea of a price range, approximate location, and amenities of the apartment before you start visiting. If you want only a place nearer town than the campus, don't start looking on the side distant from town. If air conditioning is a must, ask about this before you make an appointment to view the apartment.

Apart from the classified sections (of the school and local papers), and the accommodation office, you can get recommendations from other students; although you're probably more likely to be doing this after your freshman year, when you'll have a lot more contacts and potential roommates. Also, if you've got a neighborhood in mind, look for, "For Rent" signs in front of houses and apartments, and, of course, check online resources like CraigsList (www.craigslist.com) in the area.

When it comes to looking at apartments, if possible, visit with all your roommates at the same time. Then the group of you can make a decision about renting almost immediately. If this is not possible, elect a delegate (or two), and agree on what you absolutely can't live without, and empower them to make the decision on the spot for the group.

Cost will probably be a major factor when you and your roommates choose to live off campus. Other items to consider include several of the things discussed in the dorm section, but you might want to think about these questions as well:

- Size of the rooms (and if they are different sizes, who has to share, who gets the biggest room—and pays a different rent—and so on!)
- View from the windows
- Distance from campus
- Nearest laundry facilities, as well as shops for groceries and other supplies, places to eat, and so on
- Availability of parking, if needed
- Safety of the area, and the travel route to campus
- Part-time job opportunities locally (restaurants, offices, hospitals, and so on)

When it does come to costs, there are—again!—a number of variables. You and your roommates may want the amenities you are used to, like microwave, dishwasher, disposal, high-speed Internet, cable, air conditioning, modern baths, parking. You might get them, but you're usually going to pay for them, which is a good reason for sharing; it usually works out to be more economical.

Other plus points about sharing are the social side: you meet other people, have greater security, probably reduce what you need to spend, and maybe get more amenities. If you get a group house, there's probably going to be more space (although it may be communal). You've also got the scope to economize in other ways, like having somebody around who can fix cars, plumbing, and so on, and you can trade skills and pitch in, which can be fun as well as economical. Obviously, there are also potential downsides to sharing, which we'll come to!

Check what utilities are covered in the rent; you don't want to sort out who pays what and have a detailed budget and at the end of the month get an electricity or water bill that you didn't expect and that blows all your careful calculations out of the water.

Some landlords offer student-specific (academic-year-only) leases, which can be a saving if you're not there in the vacations. However, longer leases are usually cheaper, so if you know you're going to be there for a few years (if you're planning postgraduate study, for example), that can be worth looking into.

Talking of leases, some landlords won't rent to students without a cosigner (usually a parent) on the lease. Again, this may be a time to talk to the parents. And it's useful to make sure all the roomies' names are on the lease and other documents so nobody gets stiffed if there's a dispute.

And then you get to practical issues, which are useful to settle (at least in outline) before you sign the lease.

Many of these are exactly the same as you'll face (or have faced) in a college dorm. I've listed a few common issues below, but remember, off campus it's up to you to work out the deal. In a dorm room, you'll potentially have a residence hall adviser to help and possibly act as referee; off campus, you're on your own. So if you've been in the dorm room, ask for ideas of issues to be sorted out; it's hard to have too much information or too much awareness of what might cause friction!

- Who will take out the trash?
- Can you have visitors? Overnight guests?
- Can you play music or watch movies late at night? How late and how loud?
- Will you have a firm time for lights-out in the bedroom or common rooms? This becomes an issue if your television and computers are in the same room as anybody's bed.
- Can you borrow your roommates' clothes? Music? Computers?
- How will you decorate your room?

But as mentioned, you've got more responsibility off campus. Who will be in charge of sending the rent and utility checks each month? Do you have enough furniture? Is all of the food in the refrigerator for sharing, is it labeled, do you each have a shelf? Who gets to choose how to decorate the common areas? Who does the work and who pays for it? Who reports any problems to the landlord? Who is responsible for checking and stocking up on items like cleaning materials?

Those things need to be organized—or you'll be heading for trouble.

You don't have to be best buddies with your roommates (in the dorm or off campus) or go around together all the time, but it's generally unpleasant if you really clash. People being people, it's usually not major things, but small irritants that end up being a problem. I've known fist fights to start over things like squeezing toothpaste from the middle of the tube, forgetting to buy toilet roll (unlike at home, there is no magical fairy who deals with this and buys washing powder, and other supplies), or leaving shoes in the middle of the common area where people trip over them in the night.

So right from the start—or preferably, before you even move in—sort out how things will work, and keep up the dialogue. Be honest with your roommates about what you can stand and what drives you nuts, and urge your roommates to be candid, too.

People aren't going to change fundamentally, so a slob is going to be a slob and a neat freak a neat freak, but if you talk things out, you can usually find a compromise that works. You can't dictate how your roommates will live, and they can't make demands of you, but you can usually reach an agreement, with a dose of good temper and a sense of humor!

For example, you might have a list of chores written up so each person takes turns vacuuming the carpet and cleaning the toilet. Talk to your roommates about how it will work and do what works for *you* all, not what somebody tells you ought to. After all, you're in this together; you'll all get more value, for less money, and probably have more fun, by sharing the responsibilities. The alternative is either live alone (almost certainly more expensive) or go back into the dorm (probably easier, but with less freedom).

A potential option mentioned earlier is somebody—probably your parents—buying an investment property. That allows you to stay there, with others, and the rental income gives the property owners a return on their investment. This *can* work out very well. Clearly, this is dependent on a lot of variables: your parents (or another relative or family friend) must have the investment capital available and be willing to tie it up for at least the time you're at college, they've got to be confident you and your buddies will be paying the rents regularly (who wants to have to start debt recovery proceedings in those circumstances), it's got to work out in a way that the rents are affordable, and so on. If it does look a possibility, talk it over, and make sure that there is an accountant involved to check out the various angles.

Remember, if this does look feasible, as with everything to do with housing, you are the one who needs to drive it through—it's for your benefit, to get you the sort of place you want to live in, to do the course you want to do, in the area where you want to do it.

## SUMMARY

You've got three major choices: home, campus accommodation, off campus.

Work out what you ideally want, and see what that costs—you will probably need to make some compromises so make sure they're ones that you can live with.

Visit the campus if you can, and ask a lot of questions; it's hard to have too much information about where you may be living for four years.

Check the difference between rules and what most people do, and make your decisions accordingly.

Negotiate with potential roommates as soon as possible; set out some ground rules and agreements that you can all live with. Revisit those agreements periodically to make sure they are still relevant. If they are not, negotiate new agreements.

# Chapter 5

# Necessary Expenses

I said in Chapter 3 that it's pretty obvious that you should devote money to needs before wants—the usual "wow, how insightful" comment that people make about money. I'll let you in on a secret. I nearly did the same thing. This chapter was going to be called Living Expenses and the next one Luxuries. And I realized I was falling into the trap most people do—assuming that there are things that are universal needs ("living") and universal wants ("luxury"). It shows how easy it is to get into that mindset, to believe that money story, despite it being total nonsense!

So let's start by saying that there are very few necessary expenses in general. Most expenses are optional expenses. You *need* food, water, and shelter; that's actually pretty much all. You've got a right under the Constitution to life, liberty, and the pursuit of happiness—but as long as you have food, water, and shelter, you're alive, and if you are reading this book, you can get on and pursue happiness. Remember however, that while you're guaranteed to be able to pursue it, happiness itself isn't guaranteed, although if you follow the advice in Chapter 1 it's likely you'll get at least a fair share!

Many people think that we all need (and often have a right to) many other things from a well-paying job (or any job at all), through all the luxury food we can stuff down, to a house full of electrical and mechanical wonders that our great-grandparents never even dreamed could exist, like dishwashers, plasma TV, cell phones, and hi-speed Internet. But people do without all of those things; in fact *everybody* did without them up until less than two or three generations ago. You don't actually need them, you might want them, but that's not the same thing.

You *need* food and shelter. Beyond that, there will be things that you feel are *necessary*—like clothes—to get where you want to go, to be happy, to achieve your goals. And some of them will be unique to you, certainly the particular combination of your necessities will be unique. Your friends, your parents, nobody else will have those same exact needs; they won't have the same idea of what is *necessary* as you do, because their values, their goals, are not the same as yours and they are not you.

So in this chapter, we'll look at how you decide what it is that is necessary *for you*, and in the next chapter, we'll look at what for you are optional extras (which you might want a lot, but you don't actually *have* to have).

We looked at some of the issues around shelter in the last chapter, and we'll have another look at dealing with the expenses that go with it, to keep a roof over your head, later on. After that, we'll start to look at some of the other expenses and give you a framework for sorting out what is necessary for *you* and have a bit of a discussion about deciding among options (designer clothes? secondhand?). But first let's look at the other big need, food.

## FOOD

You're smart enough to know that having a healthy diet and getting some exercise are vital to both your physical and mental health. I said in Chapter 3 that a modern problem with food is that we evolved to hunt it down or collect it, burn a lot of energy doing that, and often have trouble finding enough food to fuel our exertions. That's why we have taste buds for sweet and umami (the savory flavor); it indicates we've got carbohydrates and protein, which our body needs so we know to eat more of them. Also, the diet we evolved for was high in vegetables, which have a lot of potassium and we needed sodium to balance that, particularly as we'd sweat out sodium running around. So we also have taste buds for salt. Consequently, you might, like a lot of people, be very fond of ice cream, pizza, fries, and other foods that are sweet, savory, and/or salty. And college, away from parents telling you to "finish off your greens; they're good for you," might seem the perfect place to eat what you like.

Obviously, you can do that if you want but make it a conscious choice if you do. Warren Buffett loves burgers and coke, but since he's still active and sharp as a tack in his 80s and can clearly afford to eat whatever he wants, he's entitled. You're entitled too, but only if you're prepared to pay for that sort of diet, in terms of money, and health! And it's not just physical health. There's increasing evidence that the quality of decisions goes down with fatigue, poor nutrition, and so on (try Googling "decision fatigue" in the *New York Times*). So if you want to make the best decisions, whether it's where to live, what to eat, which party to go to, or how to tackle a question in your midterm, you'll make better choices with better nutrition. Apart from fast foods, you've got a basic choice of eating out, eating in the college cafeteria(s), and preparing food yourself.

At college, you will be able to buy a *college food plan*. This is something else that's worth asking about when you visit. Depending on the prepaid plan you choose, you can eat a set number of meals through your college's dining service. Colleges have different set numbers, but as examples, one plan may be 10 meals per week; another may be 19.

Choose the food plan that best fits your schedule and priorities. If you buy a plan with too few meals, you will have to find food off campus, buy a single meal at the commons—both of which can be more expensive—or cook yourself. If you choose a plan with too many meals and don't use them, you probably won't get a refund for the meals you don't use.

You may know your own food preferences and dietary needs. If you don't, find out how easy it is to switch plans—and how often you can make a change—and try one plan to see how it works. Check out what your options are, and look at how you can get the diet that you need and want.

If you are looking at *eating out* other than the cafeteria, you may not need even to go off campus to get variety. The student union may have meal options, and there are probably also restaurants within walking distance. If you want more variety, there are usually (particularly around cities) a range of different cuisines.

The thing to ask yourself is whether what you're doing is eating in order to be fit and healthy, eating to enjoy the experience of eating, or eating because it's a time to socialize. You probably don't need to have the authentic cuisine of the Orient (for example), with its higher price tag, just to get the proper balance of nutrients. You may want that experience, to share it with friends (or a particular friend), to celebrate something, or other reasons. And there's nothing wrong with that. In the "food" category, options range from basic to lavish, and these days, campuses have more options of food type and availability (there's usually at least one 24 hour option). So when you choose your food plan, consider both your daily and your "special occasion" eating. That way you don't spend more than you mean to, or have to keep going for more and more exotic (and expensive) meals in order to get any variety.

If you live off campus or have a refrigerator and/or microwave in your college dorm room, you can *make meals at home*. Remember to check your dorm's policy about what types of kitchen equipment you can use in your room. Your dorm may also have a shared kitchen you can use for cooking. And be sure to consider where you have to go to get food and how often. If the nearest grocery is the most expensive, and the budget grocer is a bus or car ride away (and the schedule doesn't fit your class schedule or you don't have a car), this option may not end up saving you money. Again, consider the variables, find out when/how often you can change, and try it to see if it will add to your living experience.

If you like to cook, preparing your own meals can be economical. You can buy ingredients in bulk (which is cheaper), in season (when they are cheaper and tend to have higher vitamin content). You can make better use of fuel in that way (you're cooking larger quantities and perhaps two or three dishes at once), make more than enough, and store the excess in freezer boxes for healthy and cheap "ready meals." You can cook with friends, which can be a nice social experience and also a great deal cheaper. You can also teach one another your own favorite dishes, share the costs (so it's easier to buy and cook in bulk) and have fun, learn some skills, and eat healthier because you know the quality of the product.

The most relevant point here, it can save significant amounts of money over the year. The money you don't spend on buying ready prepared meals can fund other things you want to do.

However you do it, you'll be spending some money on food, apart from meals in the cafeteria or at restaurants. There will be things you buy for home (such as ingredients) and snacks, sandwiches, and coffees (or whatever beverage you drink).

We generally approve of ignoring those small expenses. We say people who think about small amounts are "petty" or "penny pinching" and we tend to snigger at them. And people who don't bother much about small amounts are thought of as visionary and forward looking; we admire them. Meet Art. He's a guy who is good at the "big picture." He works out regularly and doesn't want to run short on energy, so if he's hungry, he'll have a snack. He's a sociable guy and if he's chatting to friends, he'll tend to suggest having a coffee and perhaps something to nibble on, as a way to build the relationship. And he's interested in world events, so he has online subscriptions to publications like *Time* and *Forbes*, and he'll often get other papers or magazines that catch his eye. He doesn't worry about those costs; they're only a few dollars at most, often only cents, and that isn't a lot of money compared to his tuition, rent, and main food bills.

There's nothing wrong with doing that, but Art started to find he was having trouble at the end of the month paying his rent. He couldn't work out where the money was going—he'd budgeted for all the major expenses, he'd got a "social budget" (we'll talk about that in the next chapter), he never spent more than $5 without knowing it would fit into the budget—so where was the money going?

You'll have realized, and he did too, as soon as we talked about it. The occasional magazine, the newspapers that caught his eye, the coffees, the snacks, they didn't cost much, a dollar or two at a time, really small amounts. But they were spent every day, often three or four times a day. So Art might spend seven or eight dollars a day, seven days a week. That's $200+ a month.

It's very easy to do that, so it's very common for people (of all ages) to be really careful about major expenses and forget about small amounts. And they find that they've budgeted carefully for the big, one-off $1,000 expenses and forgotten about the $2–3,000 a year they spend on small amounts.

The solution is pretty simple, as Art found when we talked about it. He just budgeted for some minor expenses each day, so that he could keep track of where the money was going. He still snacked, socialized, and read, but he was more attentive to how the little amounts were important in the big picture.

This again shows how unconscious most of our decisions are; even small things, like stopping for a coffee in the morning, are a choice. You will want to find the balance that works for you between being careful with money, and having no fun at all, or appearing to be stingy to your friends. And that's fine; you don't need to live like a monk or a nun. Just be aware that you're always making choices about what to do. If you are aware, you can make sure the money goes where it will really help you—if you aren't aware, you can easily get to be like Art and find that those unconscious decisions are making a mockery of your budgeting.

The idea here is to make it easy for you to set your *own* priorities and to distinguish what is necessary for *you*—whether it's to live, to have fun, to be with your friends, to study effectively or whatever—and what might be nice to have but that might mean that you can't afford something down the road that suits your goals. And that depends on what *you* want, what is really important to *you*. I don't want you to look back and think "I should have … "; I want you to look back and say "I did … "

## HOUSING COSTS

As with the food choices, you've got a huge range of things that you *can* spend your money on. Your rent will probably (certainly if you're off campus) depend on what facilities you have, and you've probably got a choice, for example shared dorms, shared facilities, and so on.

All you *need* is shelter, although clearly there are some limits put on by the college, your landlord, and so on! But you may well have several other wants; things that you'd like to have that, for your time at college (or at least for this year or semester), are *necessary*. An example would be air conditioning. In some parts of the country, at some times of the year, you might find it's impossible to study or work because you're just too hot. Strictly, the air conditioning is optional, and for some people who can tolerate the heat, it might be. But for you, it's necessary, because without it you'll not get any work done and will end up flunking out. So again, it comes down to what *you* need.

I've made some lists of what you might have to pay for. They won't all apply to you, but if you check off the lists (I'll provide lists for other areas of expense), you can make sure you are aware of what bills you might have to pay. You can check any that are unclear with your landlord, the college, or whoever and make sure your budget (and perhaps the group budget if you're in a dorm or sharing a place off campus) covers everything and you don't get a sudden unpleasant surprise.

- Rent
- Taxes (if applicable)
- Buildings & Contents Insurance or Renter's Insurance
- Utilities
  - Electric
  - Water
  - Oil or gas
- Maintenance (plumbing, electrical work, carpentry, and so on)
- Cleaning products and other consumables (polish, dishwasher and washing liquids, toilet paper, and so on)
- Durables (dishcloths, mop, buckets, and so on)
- Phone (landline and/or mobile)
- Internet link
- Satellite/digital subscription
- Deposit, or insurance for potential property damage
- Garden maintenance (fuel for mower and so on)

There are ways to economize on most of those, which we'll talk about as we go on and get to specifics of keeping to a budget. But if you think about these items and factor them into your housing costs, you are likely to be prepared in an emergency.

One thing to be clear about before you sign a lease is whether utilities— electricity, gas, water—are included in the monthly cost or extra. If you pay them, it's to your benefit (and your roommates) to budget for them and make sure you have the money on hand to pay the bills (or prepay them). Even if you don't have to pay directly (because it's included in the rent or because you are living at home), it makes sense to be aware of the energy you are using and not waste it. There are masses of websites with tips about how to save money, but here are some basics.

In general:

- Turn off the lights when you go to bed or there's nobody in a room.
- Turn down room and water thermostats a degree or two.
- Don't leave appliances on standby; turn them off at the socket when not in use. If any lights are on in electrical equipment, then it's still using electricity.
- Don't leave laptops and mobile phones on charge unnecessarily; they only need a couple of hours.

With clothes and washing:

- If possible, fill up the washing machine, tumble dryer, or dishwasher: One full load uses less energy than two half loads.
- Wash clothes at lower temperatures. Modern washing powders and detergents work just as effectively at lower temperatures, and it can be worth buying clothes that specifically you can wash like that (and preferably not have to have dry cleaned!).
- Wear a sweater in the house if you're cold, rather than turn up the heating!

In the kitchen:

- Boil only the water you need in your kettle, and de-scale it from time to time (there are lots of tips on the Internet on how to do this).
- Check what you have in the fridge and freezer before you go shopping. Wasted food is a big contributor toward carbon dioxide emissions as well as wasting money.
- Cut food into smaller pieces to speed up the cooking time.
- Use the right sized pan for the job and right sized hob ring for each pan.

- Keep lids on pans as much as you can, to reduce heat loss—turn the heat down when it reaches the boil.
- Keep the oven door shut as much as possible; make sure the glass door is clean so you can see what's going on.
- Let warm foods cool down before putting them in the fridge.
- Make sure air can circulate around the back of your fridge and freezer.
- Make sure your fridge and freezer are set to the right temperature.
- Don't keep the fridge or freezer door open for longer than necessary.
- Try not to put the fridge or freezer next to a heat source such as a cooker or radiator, or in direct sunlight.
- Defrost food in the fridge overnight rather than microwaving it.
- Use a microwave to reheat food where possible as this is usually a much more efficient method of warming things up than using the hob or oven.
- Cover food with a microwave-safe lid or pierced cling film to hold moisture and speed up cooking times in the microwave.

You can save a lot of money just doing those sort of simple things. And it's money that you then have available for stuff you want—you are making your choice!

We've talked about "shelter," and we've talked about "food." As you're going to college, there are some other costs that you can't avoid, namely:

## COLLEGE COSTS

You're going to college, so we can take that as necessary! And there are costs for that which you can't realistically avoid. Here's a list:

- Tuition fees
- Health insurance
- Books
- Visits
- Workshop equipment and so on

A few notes on these.

We'll talk about various forms of insurance later, including the contents and perhaps buildings cover that you probably need for off campus living that were in the list for housing costs.

But you are required to have health insurance for college. In some areas you have to provide proof of cover, and you may automatically be charged for insurance unless it has officially been waived. So if you're covered on your parents' plan, get the details such as finding out how long that coverage extends. In some cases it can last until you (as a dependent) are in your mid-20s and have finished college. So, with luck, you may end up with a better plan without spending anything at all. If not, the college will usually provide a carrier, and although the costs and cover vary, they're usually less expensive than private plans. Find out, because although they are usually less expensive (and are therefore more basic in what is provided), you can use another insurer or policy, so check it out and get what works best for you.

Because your health is important and there might be particular things you need that aren't covered within the policy, you might also want to look at optical, dental, and any complimentary therapy bills and check the services offered at the college health services.

Getting *books* can be a big expense (depending on the reading list you have). This is another difference from high school. There you often get the texts provided and the reading lists are small and more manageable. At college, you have to get the books yourself (your professors will tell you what to read, not where to get it), you can have immense reading lists (one psychology lecture list I had ran to about eight core and thirty plus "useful" chapters and articles, plus three popular science books as "background!"), and if you want to do well, you need to do at least the core reading. If you've followed the ideas so far, you'll be really interested in the subject, so you'll want to do some of the subsidiary reading as well.

There are several options. The cheapest is the library, which is one of the reasons that in talking about Terri in Chapter 1 I mentioned that she wanted to make friends with the librarian and the other "gatekeepers." Being able to get copies of articles from Journals is actually as helpful as borrowing books (if you are serious about the subject, the professional articles are the real meat of the subject in academic terms), and realistically the college (and other) libraries are the major sources of these. It's not feasible for most people to afford all the professional Journals that could be useful, not while they are students. It isn't all perfect with a library, of course. You may only be able to borrow it for a few weeks, not the whole term, and libraries take a dim view of making notes in the margin or underlining passages (I don't recommend—or condone—anybody doing this: Library books are to be shared, after all!). If you're in a position to read novels or general texts (if you're reading English, say, or history), you might be able to get what you want, but with most subjects the college library has only a limited number of copies, and you have to look elsewhere. So don't forget the city and county libraries (or even your hometown one—you never know). The Internet has expanded the resources available to most libraries, so get to know your online resources, talk to the librarian, and poke about a bit on your own.

If you're buying books (which is useful for core texts, particularly), you *can* get them at the campus bookstore. They will stock the main items (and a lot of the options) for the semester because the professors will give them copies of the reading lists. That makes them convenient—which like most convenience (having better room facilities, luxury food, or comprehensive insurance) comes at a price.

As I've said before, this is *your* choice. If you want convenience, you can just rock up to the campus bookstore at the start of the semester and buy all you want. But be aware that what you spend there will no longer be available to you for the room, for food, for entertainment.

So here are some alternatives. See if the bookstore has the books *secondhand*. They obviously aren't pristine, but they do the job—as long as you can get the right edition. Have a look at the books before you buy: Some people actually prefer used textbooks, because they often have key passages underlined and highlighted, as well as notes from the previous owner. That can be a help; it's actually so commonly done that it's a key feature of the Harry Potter story, *The Half-Blood Prince!* I have my own idiosyncrasies with notes and highlighting, and I find other people's notes distracting—but it's what *you* want, what works for *you*.

Even secondhand the campus bookstore still might be more than you want to (or can) afford. Look *online*. Websites and forums often sell both new and used college textbooks cheaper than the campus bookstore. Compare prices when you choose your courses and see where you can get the best deal. This might lead you to another source of books, and potentially one of the cheapest, buy from a previous student (at your college, or another one). The simplest is to buy from a student who took the course the previous year, or semester. It's a win-win; you get a better deal and the other student gets more money than the bookstore would normally offer. You may find offers of books on notice boards, around the student's union, or in local student hangouts (like coffee shops). Again, make sure you are buying the right edition for your course. A newer edition may have minor updates; see if you can find out whether that will affect your learning.

You can also raise money for the next semester's books by selling last semester's! If you're going to do that, make sure you sell them immediately after you've finished with the book. The college bookstore will reimburse you part of the price if the textbook will be used during the next term (check the policy at your bookstore). As with buying the books, you may be able to ask a higher price from other students, either via cards on notice-boards and so on (or even via helpful professors who arrange to link up buyers and sellers in their classes—but don't count on that one) or by selling your textbooks online to students at other colleges. The reason for selling them quickly, if you're going to, is that the professor could switch texts or there may be a new edition available, which will leave you stuck with the old version. You might sell it online, as other colleges may not have updated, but it's not a sure thing as if your professor doesn't want students using the older version, other professors probably won't either.

Again, it's all down to what you *want*. I like books and articles, and along with all the other professional ones I've bought over the years, I still have several of my basic texts from my finance exams, my psychology degree, masters, and so on. That's my choice; yours may be different, but be aware that it is a choice. Buying, selling, borrowing, lending, and generally dealing in books are ways to get the information that you need to learn the subjects you want to learn. The amount of money and time it costs you, and the number of books you end up with, are your choices.

The same thing applies with any materials you are expected to supply for projects, copying of papers, any visits you want to make. It's possible to economize on these things (we'll talk about transport and visits shortly), but you have to decide what it is you want and what you're prepared to give up in terms of other things, in order to get it.

One other thing that you might feel is necessary—but that's often over-looked—is:

- Regular charity donation

It's one of the things that's strongly linked in the research on happiness —helping others makes you happier. You might really not have the money to contribute financially at college (even if you have done in the past)—but it's worth at least considering doing something for a good cause you care about or giving some voluntary time. If you've done any voluntary work, sports coaching, helping people or animals, or anything similar, you'll know the personal fulfillment you get from it. There may be volunteer programs run through the college, but in any case, it's worth giving some thought to making a contribution of time and/or money, in terms of the value to you in happiness and contributing to the world.

## TRAVEL

One of the things people tend to think is "necessary" at college is a car—and for you it might be. But it does come with various costs, for example:

- Gas
- Car insurance
- Registration
- Inspection
- Parts (tires, oil, wiper blades, batteries, and so on)
- Replacements (shocks, exhaust system, brake pads and disks, and so on)
- Maintenance (garage costs) or DIY
- Breakdown cover
- Parking

This is where roommates and other friends can be helpful. It's not just in terms of a "designated driver," for one night's party; it allows you to cut down on the expenses of everybody having to pay all the expense of having separate cars. It's something that you need to negotiate (who gets the car on Saturday night if you're going to different places!), but there are economies that can be made.

Similarly, as I mentioned about housing costs and DIY, you may be able to do trades on work. If you're a good mechanic, is this a skill that you can trade, not for money but for convenience like the use of a car, fixing a friend's car in return for some improvements on your property, for a meal or two, and similar trades? You can have a whole trade economy with tokens and the like, and I'll say a bit more about that in the next chapter—but the main point is that in order to afford things you may want (like a car), you can either reduce the cost in some way or generate some extra income to cover it. Trading is a way to produce either.

There are obviously alternative forms of transport. There may be a public transit system (on which you may get a student discount); if there are services such as student shuttle services, they will usually be cheap (or free) but may not be so convenient in some situations. Some campuses now have Zipcar service, which allows you to rent a car for a short time to do errands or go out to dinner—and is a good alternative to full-time ownership.

You can also bike around campus. It's a one-time investment, unless you've already got a bike, but you do need to get a good lock, and you will probably need repairs at some point. Some campuses now have free bike share services, allowing you to pick up a bike, ride from Point A to Point B, and secure the bike at Point B, waiting for another rider.

If you are going to a college in another state, you probably need to plan for airplane, bus, or train tickets home during the holidays—unless you plan on driving (which has gas and potentially overnight costs for the journey) or getting a ride with a college mate who has a car—in which case you also need to factor in gas, tolls, or other travel costs.

So there are some other aspects that may need to feature in your budget if you're not going to have a car.

- Fares for public transport and shuttle
- Cycle purchase, lock, secure storage
- Cab fares
- Travel between college and home

One other point about necessary expense: It applies to optional ones as well, and I'll say more about it in the next chapter, but bear in mind the functional quality of what you buy.

If you buy anything, necessary or not, make sure it's the right item for your purpose. If name brand is important to you, or you have experience of it being dependable, by all means, rely on your experience. Sometimes the cheapest alternative is actually the most expensive because the item doesn't last, the tool doesn't work, the shirt doesn't fit—you get my drift. The marketing industry is set up to exploit the tendency to do what we've always done and not question it, to make rapid decisions (such as "buy X brand—we always get that").

So test things out (with your roommates if appropriate), ask around, read reviews, and check the functional quality of what you buy. You might try budget brands, the store's own lines, small local organizations' services as distinct from big franchises. See what works. If you find that nobody actually likes the cheap stuff, or find that, for example, the food is stiff with sugar and artificial preservatives, don't buy it because it is cheap. Run brand tests; is the supermarket's own brand distinguishable from the one we usually buy at home? Interview your roommates and see if the washing liquid works better, worse, or the same as the one you've been buying because of habit.

The idea is to economize on things without sacrificing quality and to judge the quality by what you value—not on the label or the price tag. In this way, you are also developing your own system for figuring out what works for you.

When you've got the necessary items budgeted for, it's a wise move to set up regular payments into accounts to make sure that everything is covered. I'll say more about this in future chapters, but if you have your money going into an account and immediately the appropriate amount comes out for your housing, household bills, food, and any other essentials, you've got the bills covered. You probably won't have any trouble spending what you've got left—but you won't be spending money that you want for things that are important to you.

## SUMMARY

There's a limit to what you really need: The essentials are food, shelter, and college expenses.

Everything else is a choice—it might be essential for you, but somebody else might not care. Others might spend their money on things that you don't care about—and likewise, they may question your spending choices. So you decide what is a "necessary" expense for you and ignore what anybody else does or thinks.

Make sure you've got all the necessary expenses covered—the lists in the chapter are there to help you.

Set a budget for your necessary expenses and put money aside for it. You'll easily spend any money left over after necessary expenses, but if you try to cover the expenses from what you have left over after you've spent, you probably won't have enough left!

And don't forget the odd small amounts that you pay; they can add up to a lot. Just as an experiment, try paying cash for your everyday expenses for a week and see how aware you become!

Chapter 6

# Optional Expenses

As I said in the last chapter, most expenses are optional when you come right down to it, which would mean that this chapter could end up really long!

But you don't need to read a huge tome, listing all sorts of do's and don'ts. You just need some ideas and some principles so you can make decisions that work for you, and some tools to help you figure out what's worth spending your money on—and where you want to economize.

So let's have a look at some principles to help you make decisions.

## OPPORTUNITY COST

That's a fancy name for what you give up by making any decision—you could have made a different one. You've already considered one decision: which college to go to. If you choose the relative freedom of one far from home (away from parental eyes!), you give up the convenience and lower cost of being at home. Any choice you make about good things (opportunities for study with great professors, interesting parts of the country, campus life, anything you can think of) means you have to give up something else. Even with small, often unconscious decisions—like Art spending money on snacks with friends—you are making decisions about trade-offs, because you have a finite pool of funds you are working with.

So it's worth remembering that each choice you make means that you can't spend the time, money, or other resource on something else. If you go to one party, you can't go to the other one at the same time; if you work out, you can't be studying or socializing at the same time.

This isn't something to be scared of; you can handle it. You just benefit from being aware of it and taking it into account. Now you are aware, tell me, what makes more sense for handling your money?

Choice A. Decide what you really want, spend your money on those things, then see how much is left and maybe buy some other things that you want a bit less.

Choice B. Spend your money on whatever you want at the time, what your friends have, what somebody tells you that you ought to have, irrespective of whether you want it the most and whether, in fact, you want it at all.

Remember, the opportunity cost principle says you can't do both. If you spend on something now, when you have a choice you prefer in the future, you don't have the funds—so you've foregone your best alternative. You may say the first choice was better—but was that because it was the first choice you had to make, or was it really better? If both options had been presented at the same time, would you still choose the one you did? You chose without being aware of how often you are making choices and—until now—of the opportunity cost principle.

### BUILD IN THE FUN STUFF

This goes back to your goals and the necessary expenses. You obviously (opportunity cost) want to have your rent, college fees, and food covered. You also want to have any other necessary expenses (for you) taken care of. Those are going to be the first things that are in your budget—the foundation.

That's going to be your option A choices; the expenses that are most important, which we've referred to before as "needs." Another "need," as we said in the last chapter, includes transport of some form—unless you live close enough to walk (you may have decided that paying higher rent would save transport cost. See how this works?).

You'll know what your "needs" are and you'll know what money you've got overall, from any job, scholarship, grant, and so on. Taking one from the other gives you the amount you've got for optional expenses, or "wants."

It's usually a help to plan in some "fun" with that money. That's what I referred to earlier as a "social budget"; it's the stuff that isn't absolutely must-have—but it's really important for actually living your life and enjoying it!

Maybe you really, really like clothes—I don't mean functional ones just to avoid having to go to lectures naked—I mean clothes (or shoes, or accessories, or all of them) that make you feel good about yourself. In that case, it makes sense to budget yourself a regular clothing allowance.

Maybe you like eating different cuisine—so you would benefit from an interesting food allowance.

Whatever it is that you know will make you feel good, that's what is "fun" and that's what it is helpful to budget for. Think about it as giving yourself an allowance. It can be as much or as little as you want—but it's got to fit in with the opportunity cost principle. So you want to build in the fun stuff, all of it, at the start. If you like clothes, and like to party, and like to experiment with different food, you have to make decisions about how much you can spend on each and set that money aside.

If you've never budgeted before, you may need to experiment with the amount: Reserve the "needs"; then try different amounts for the "wants." At different times of the year, you may spend different amounts (that once a year sale at your favorite store, holiday parties, summer vacations). Try to look ahead and anticipate what is coming up as you decide what amounts you might spend in each category.

Remember option B. If you just think "I've got a couple of parties and I want some new clothes for them and I don't want to give up my regular social life"—you'll end up having spent all the money and might have nothing for the essential stuff that is actually what you need the most.

## BEWARE OF PSYCHOLOGY!

You might think that you are always the one who makes decisions on what you buy, how much, what brand, and so on. In the end, you are, but retailers and advertisers are getting increasingly clever about influencing your decision and creating urgency (watch your e-mail for a week and see how many "last chance sale" notices you get *from the same store.* How "last chance" can it be!)

A lot of this book is about how your mind works and how you behave, especially given certain cues. I've mentioned research into actual human behavior, not in laboratories but in real-life situations. The science of that human behavior is psychology, and that's what I've studied (and teach), so that's why I know about it. But I'm not the only guy who knows!

Let's look at some examples of the ways you are being influenced to make a decision to spend money.

### Stores

The model here is supermarkets.

If you walk past a supermarket, you'll see things like fruit and vegetables, healthy drinks, things that make your subconscious think, "that's good, I ought to get some of that." It might be hot, you might be peckish, but there's a little bit of "I ought to eat more fresh stuff," whether you're actually hungry or thirsty or you aren't.

If you go in, you have to walk past shelves. And if you are simply after a single product, it's probably a staple, something like bread or milk—which will be at the back, as far away from the entrance as possible. That means you have to walk past a lot of shelves.

That's already exposed you to the human tendency to want things we see, that are available, things like chips and dip—"see it and pick it up because suddenly it's attractive" purchases. But there's a lot more.

Items to appeal to men will be shelved a couple of inches above those designed to appeal to women—because there is a difference in average heights, and most people look at (and are therefore more likely to buy) items at their eye level. Those items that you see easily, and can reach without bending or stretching, will be the ones that have the highest mark up because they represent the highest profit for the store. They're the ones that research studies (and store returns) show are the ones that get bought far more than the ones that you need to look up or down even to see, and that you need to bend or stretch to reach.

If you happen to take children into a supermarket, the items that will cause them to have a tantrum until you buy them whatever it is out of sheer embarrassment will be at the children's eye level; you won't even see it in time to divert their attention from it!

So with any item, from a can of beans to a toilet brush, the one you see first will be the ones with the high margin. The alternative with the lower margin will be harder to see, harder to find (it may not even be on display until the store has shifted the stuff it wants to shift), harder to reach and won't necessarily be labeled clearly. The items the store really wants to shift fast (maybe ones nearing a sell-by date) will be at the end of rows, where people with trolleys have to slow down and are more likely to spot a "bargain."

So unless you are conscious of what is going on, the store gets a higher profit margin on each item and you pay more than you need.

And, of course, many items that you bought you didn't intend to buy at all—you only went in for some bread, remember!

Another store idea is the "special offer"—psychologically, we like to feel we're getting something for nothing. So stores will offer things like "buy one and get one free" (known as BOGO), and you may actually end up spending more when you think you're saving. Check it out by looking at the price per unit. In most groceries, there is a tag on the shelf that lists the price of the item as well as the price per unit (pound, liter, gallon, and so on). Compare the price per unit measure on two items— one looks like a deal, one looks expensive—to see if it really is. There are several ways that ploy works. One is that you may buy because of the "free" element, but actually you may not even use the one you pay for, let alone the two you get. If you didn't really need one, why buy two just because one is "free?"

Another way that a "special offer" works is that it focuses you on what you seem to be saving, when actually you need to focus on what you are spending. If you've got $50 available and you spend $100, even if the offer allows you to buy $300 worth of goods for that $100, you're still down $50, not in credit $200. But you saw the $200 you "saved." That's how the mind works. It takes effort to think of the money spent, not the money "saved."

Often, you'll be encouraged to buy on credit, because it's been shown that people spend more on credit cards.[1] We'll talk more about credit cards in the next chapter, but beware of them because, whatever you think you'll do, you *will* spend more on a credit card than if you had to pay cash.

And although they can be a good deal if you really would use the quantity you buy, sometimes the "special offer" is only "special" in that it makes you spend especially large amounts. Make sure you work out whether a deal really is as good as it looks and if a "2 for 1" or "3 for $1" offer will actually save you money. That can require a bit of basic math, so take out your phone and use the calculator function to work out details.

You can work this to your advantage if there are items you regularly buy; stock up when there is a special offer, which may involve some planning, but make a game of it. Just make sure that it is genuinely a good offer—you'd hate to buy something thinking it was a bargain because it was on "special offer," only to find it for less at normal price in another store!

Impulse items—gum, candy, magazines, and other items offered while you are waiting in line are just that—you didn't mean to buy them but you had to wait in the checkout line, and you found an article you wanted to finish, so you spent "only" $5 on the magazine.

I could write a whole book on the ways this works, but it would be out of date by the time it was published. Data is constantly being gathered and massaged to optimize store sales (especially in supermarkets, which have razor-thin margins!) and increase inventory turnover and merchandise is moved around to catch your eye and make it easy for you to grab the highest-margin product. The essential point is to remember that you have choices about what to buy. The stores are in business to sell things, and it is good business to use sound psychology to make their business more successful. I want you to take advantage of the offers that are helpful to you, and be clear about trade-offs you are making for your benefit. All you need to do is to be aware and to make your own decisions.

### Restaurants, Cafés, Bars

When restaurants offer to "run a tab," it is both a convenience and a management tool—it usually means you will spend more. If you had to pay cash, you might decide between the appetizer and the desert because you don't have the cash available for both. But if you are paying on a credit card, you might have both because the card makes it easy. Similarly, food or drinks at half price are less about offering food than about building traffic at a slow time of day, giving you food so you'll spend more on drinks, or simply getting you into the mood to spend. Nothing wrong with that; it's sound business practice, but in this context, you are your own business too, and if you are aware of what is going on, you can make conscious business choices about how much you actually want to spend—or not (opportunity cost again).

And there is more at work than just what is on the menu: Restaurants, bars, and cafés use the ambience well. Styles, colors, shape of plates, lighting, spacing of tables, even the music can be part of the setup. For example, we associate classical music with affluence, and people spend more if that's playing, and without any music, people spend less.[2] Similarly, matching the music to the style—French music in a French restaurant—works to help people spend more, and if you have, say, Italian and French wine and play Italian music, people will drink more Italian wine! Strange but true, so if the Italian wine has a higher mark up, the cute restaurant plays Italian music; if the French is the bigger profit item, they go for French.

I've mentioned at various times that it's wise to compare prices. So often we look down menus to identify the most cost-effective items for us. That's quite easy if the prices are right justified; they all align. Of course, if the menu is center-aligned, the prices don't line up and it's more difficult to compare (guess which option many restaurants use).

Another presentation point is pictures. We are a visually dominated species; did you know a picture of a dish on a page can increase the amount you spend by up to a third, and even having dollar signs or not makes a difference, just numbers and no sign or words makes us spend more?[3]

Restaurants and cafés can also use written presentation to persuade you, in the same way as stores can use the layout. You'd assume that because we read from left to right, we'd read a menu the same way. Actually, we tend to look to the upper right-hand corner first. This is often where the "anchor," the highest price, highest profit item is. We'll say more about anchoring shortly but it does work. It also doesn't just focus us on the high-profit items (like placing things on the easy access shelves in stores). Having the relatively costly dish listed makes the other items look cheaper in comparison. Of course, the other side of this is that we tend to look at the bottom left of a menu last, so this is where the least expensive dishes will often be.

The "prix fixe" or the "combo" meals in fast-food restaurants are set up to look like good value, but actually, it makes it harder to compare prices. Similarly, the small plates for sharing are often sold as being economical, but most people spend more because they simply order more dishes. It's often worth trying to compare the prices and ordering less than you think you'll need between a group; you can always get some more if you're still hungry.

### Closing Sales

Sales training and books about selling are full of "closes"—ways of getting people to commit to buy. I was taught a lot of them when I worked in finance and they're still in use—I've just got more idea of why they work than when I learned them. I've mentioned one factor that makes people buy already—fear, the fear that we'll miss out on something that often makes people take "free offers" that aren't actually worth having. Again, I could write a book on closes, but here are a few key ones that you will encounter, so have a read and then decide whether you need or want to buy.

**"The Puppy Dog Close"**    If you want to sell a puppy, do you need glib sales talk, evidence of training, bloodline books, and so on? No, just the puppy. You take it around, show it to the customer, let the children play with it, and then you casually say "oh, the office is closed now, I'll have to put it in the kennels over the weekend." What happens? The customer (with a horde of tearful children) insists that it is no trouble, they'll look after it, and you can pick it up on Monday. On Monday, do you think they'll let you take the puppy away?

Why do you think car salesmen let you have a test drive? Once you get behind the wheel and picture yourself as Jason Bourne or Lara Croft, the car is yours. It works with any material goods, so any offer to let you "try it out," try it on, and so on is potentially going to get you to buy something that you don't necessarily want.

**"The Alternate Advance Close"**    If you're considering, say, a bag—what do you think if the sales person asks "which do you prefer, the blue or the red?" You almost certainly try to decide whether you prefer blue or red, which means you've already (unconsciously) made part of a decision to buy; you're just wondering about which color. It works with a lot of questions, which size, when do you want delivery (Tuesday or Saturday), will you take it now or collect it when you've finished shopping—all sorts of questions.

Whichever way it goes, the alternative you give has advanced you toward buying.

**"The Takeaway Close"**    This is related to fear and also pride. If you're told, "I'm not sure you can benefit from this, it's usually a more sophisticated buyer who wants it," what do you think? If somebody says, "I'm not sure you'd qualify for this product," how do you feel? You're likely to want to prove that you are "good enough," sophisticated, with the resources and maturity—you don't want to miss out on something good. It's also the basis of the "final sale" offer—if you don't buy it now, it will be taken away (yeah, sure it will!).

So instead of focusing on whether you really want it, you may switch to trying to prove to the salespersons that you are worthy of it and almost pleading with them to sell it to you!

**"The Ben Franklin Close"**    This is actually quite sophisticated psychology. Salespersons realize that you are thinking about the purchase and perhaps raising objections. So they ask (if they're good) if you know how Ben Franklin made decisions. If you aren't impressed with Ben Franklin, they find somebody who you respect as being wise and use them, but traditionally, it was Ben Franklin. Ben, allegedly, made decisions by drawing a line down a sheet of paper and writing all the reasons in favor of a decision (to buy, for example) on one side and all the reasons against (not to buy) on the other side. Then you add them up. So you've raised, let's say, two objections. They can find dozens of reasons why you ought to buy—so, they say, "the answer's pretty obvious."

I say this one is clever, because it's the way people think they make decisions, it seems logical, it's got the authority of somebody you respect behind it, what's not to like? But of course it isn't actually the way we think; we don't make that sort of logical comparisons in real life, and if you're going to use something like that anyway, you'd need to balance the "weight" of the evidence—things like the color of a computer, the screen size, the sensitivity of the touchpad, and so on might be large numbers of advantages, but they are probably not as important as the reliability, the power, or the price, any one of which might outweigh all of the minor details put together.

It's not a bad way to make decisions, but if you're going to do it, take the details away and have a good think about all of the pros and cons, and make your own decision. If somebody is using the "Ben Franklin" on you, your decision is likely to be more helpful to that person than to you—and that will cost you money.

**"The Add-On Close"**   We've talked about our tendency to ignore minor costs; this close works on increasing the value of the sale with small individually and huge collectively added items.

So "would you like the designer trim, only $5?" And "the special presentation case, only $6.50." And "you'll want the extended warranty."

Individually all those things are only 5 percent or 10 percent of the purchase, so like the coffee and magazines that Art bought, they seem insignificant. And note that each thing is treated separately. The extras aren't all run together in one sentence; each extra is treated as a single decision. You're not asked if you want to add $20 to a $50 purchase (40%); you're asked if you want $2 (4%) or $5 (10%). It's never a big percentage in one go, but you can easily add 40 percent or so to the purchase price in total. So the bigger the basic price, the more that can be added—there will be more money involved with buying a car than a phone.

When you are buying anything, think about the "add-ons" as a new item and what you'd pay for them separately. So think of the "cheap" extended warranty as a separate insurance. What would it cost to put it on your existing possessions cover? If the sunroof for your car can be added for, say, "only" eight percent work out, what you'd have paid to add it to a car you already owned (or ask your parents what they'd be prepared to pay to add one to the family car as a special item).

## COMPARE COST AND VALUE TO YOU

You've probably noticed that you buy particular items from habit because it's the brand you grew up with or because it's the "luxury brand" or because an ad has convinced you that it will (fill in the blank —make you smarter, sexier, and so on) rather than because you actually value what the product does. So you'll buy a new textbook because you like the smell of new books, not because there is actually any intrinsic advantage to it.

One idea for dealing with this is to experiment and trade down. If you always buy named brands, try a store brand item. If you buy the store brand, try the economy. Can you actually notice the difference; are your whites whiter, does the branded clothing look better or fit better?

You can pay for the label alone. That's particularly common with clothes; some people can't bear to be seen without the "right" label. If it's really important to you, if it really has value and it's something that for you is a necessary expense, or is something that you're prepared to give up other things for, that's fine. But remember the opportunity cost —if you pay extra for the label, it's money that you've chosen to pay for the label—and you may come up short on the price of the concert you have waited three years to go to.

In some cases, it is worth paying for the label, so do some research. I've found, for example, that paying less for a cashmere sweater is always a waste of money; a higher end cashmere sweater will last for years without pilling or stretching. On the other hand, I've talked about clothing to tailors trained in Savile Row, the *home* of bespoke tailoring and "a byword for quality throughout the world." They say that a lot of the mass-produced "label" brands of clothes are actually quite poorly made, the stitching is not done properly, linings are not correctly cut, and so on. It means that, often, you can get clothing that is of better quality, will fit better, last longer, and hence look better for less money if you buy on the basis of quality and fit rather than the name on the label. So it will be worth your time actually to compare stitching and finishing and remember that it doesn't cost anything to try one on—and ask questions.

The material label may mean something (as with cashmere); sadly, the brand label may not—so check it out and decide what matters to you and whether the label does indicate something that you will value and are prepared to pay for.

Remember, it is all a case of opportunity cost and your choices. If you really must have a different outfit for each day of the year, then for now you're probably going to have to do things like buy secondhand, adapt clothes yourself, or buy on the basis of value, not quality. If you want the brand labels, you probably have to accept that you can't have so many outfits—it's your decision as to what is most important and what you should spend your money on.

So what are you likely to spend your optional spending money on?

### Clothes and Accessories

You'll obviously have a wardrobe already, so it may not be a major expense to start with. But as the everyday wear gets worn or goes out of style, there will be more need/desire to replace clothes, underwear, shoes, belts, and so on.

A useful guideline is to look at "cost per use." If you're going to get a lot of wear out of something, its effective cost to you is lower. Say you'll wear it every week for a couple of years, then you will wear it about 100 times and can divide the cost by 100 to get the "cost per use." Not that you shouldn't buy the special outfit for a special event that may only get worn once (so its cost per use is its price). It just means that you need to think about what you could get for your money and how important that one event, and that one outfit, is for you.

- Personal care
- Shampoo, toothpaste, and so on
- Fitness/sports/gym
- Hairdressers
- Beauty treatments

You'll be buying personal care items for your room—some might be part of the communal budget, depending on whether you and any roommates share items, but you'll probably have some items where you want your own particular favorite products.

You may be paying for various health and fitness courses, facilities, coaching, and so on, so it's worth including those in your budget.

Tastes vary with spending on hair and beauty treatments. Some people just can't seem to live without them; others think it's a waste of money. It's up to you, but make sure you know that those expenses are accounted for, or you may get a nasty surprise at some point when you don't have the money you thought you did.

- Computer and electrical goods
- Antivirus
- Backup
- Security
- Apps

Depending on your course and personal preferences, you might want to replace your computer during your time at college. Again, it's something that you can budget for. Identity theft, loss of data (and equipment), viruses, and so on are a real threat and generally cost money, so consider your spending on security, as well as taking some common sense precautions, to avoid problems.

- Entertainment
  - DVD rental
  - Music/film downloads
  - Books, paper, or e-book
  - Computer games
  - Cinema/theater trips
  - Newspapers, magazines
  - Cigarettes
- Events
  - Christmas or other festivals
  - Holidays
  - Birthdays

A couple of points about those. You can use previous experience as a guideline. Instead of getting worried about what you *ought* to spend, check what has happened previous years and use that as a baseline for your budget.

It's useful—but not easy—to avoid birthdays and other celebrations becoming a "status race" with friends and relatives. It can end up meaning that everybody keeps buying more and more expensive items to compete. So it might sound as if it's unfriendly, unromantic, and so on, but it's a good idea to set spending limits on presents for everybody's use; that way it doesn't get to the point where everybody's budget gets blown because somebody got a bit carried away one time and it may be a relief for everyone to have guidelines on the table.

It's also useful to have a "wish list" (if you've got doting relatives, it's a great idea) that way you get stuff you really want (but maybe couldn't manage to get for yourself) and avoid getting stuff that politeness makes you say was great, but that you don't want!

## Hobbies

You probably want to fit any expenses you have for hobbies into your budget; it might not be strictly a "necessary" expense, but if you can afford to keep something going, it's often very rewarding.

There's another aspect (apart from the pleasure) from following hobbies. If you do anything creative, artistically, in computer design, sound mixing, and so on, you can give great gifts to people that are really personal and appreciated (people like the care somebody takes over them more than simply spending money on them) but that don't cost you very much and that you can have fun creating as well.

And if you do have hobbies or interests that allow you to do things others can't, you can actually supplement your budget in several ways. I referred to trades on work before, things like car repairs, altering clothes, cooking, and so on. You might just help out friends for the pleasure of helping and because you enjoy your hobby, and that's great. You might also trade directly with them; they fix your car, and you prepare them a meal or whatever. And you can spread the net a bit wider and have a token system where you exchange favors on a more commercial basis. I've seen those run successfully on several bases, on time spent, on a single job, or on the market value compared to buying the equivalent in stores. The point is that you get to do something that you would like to do for free anyway but might not be able to afford to do bearing in mind all the other demands on your budget. You also get to trade for other things you might want, food, clothes, art works, car repairs, or whatever, and get them for little or no cost compared to what you'd have to pay otherwise. One note: You may need to experiment here because though you may have a budget for hobbies, you may not have time, given new college demands on your time. Or your hobby may be a way to socialize, which doesn't involve a huge expense.

## Pet Costs

Your living situation and time may not allow you to have your own animal at school. But consider the community and, if you have time, you may be able to earn extra cash pet sitting or dog walking while on a break from studying.

To catch any other costs you might have, think about what you'd do for a fun day—and again, because college is new, you might not know at the outset. But think about what activities you'd like to do and what things you'd need to do them. That should help to make sure you've got a good idea of what you might want to buy, if the budget can stretch that far. Then you can think about how you can get it to stretch!

## Principles of Buying for Less

We tend to regard the first figure we hear as a reasonable guideline. It doesn't matter whether that figure is reasonable, or even whether it's just a random figure (seriously, Google "anchoring and adjustment" and look at the examples about the number of nations in the United Nations). Consequently, we are influenced by the first figure we hear, whether it is relevant or not. Which is why restaurants use it to "anchor" on a high price to start with.

Nobody believes they fall for this, but there are many examples, the classics being with real estate. If agents (even very experienced ones) are shown particulars of a house, they will estimate different prices depending upon the guide price they are given. Every time this is done, the agents say (and believe) they judge objectively from their experience, depending on the location, size, and other relevant factors, and ignore the guide price. Every time, they actually anchor on the price given and use it as a major (possibly the only) guide.

So if somebody gives you a price for something that first figure influences you. That's why, in bargaining, it is handy to get your estimate in first; it will influence the other person.

And although you might not have much choice (most stores won't allow you to bargain—although you can always try), you can check out what competitor prices are to give you an alternative base figure to work from. So for things like the "3 for 2" offers, check out what other people are charging. Otherwise you might fix on what the seller is asking and believe that the special offer, "happy hour," and so on discounts are real discounts from what the product is worth, rather than a hypothetical discount from a really high base figure that means you'll pay more with the benefit of the offer than you would have done without it! And before you go off to buy something, do a bit of research (or you can do some of them while you are standing in the aisle!).

**Price Comparison Sites**   All sites are usually accessible by phone and Internet and let you compare the cost of just about any major item. Also handy is the fact that these sites often contain user reviews from other customers (a classic for that is TripAdvisor). You can also use them for supermarket shopping and compare the costs of your shop across several major stores for food, health and beauty, household products, and so on. If you can keep the cost of the necessary stuff down, you've got more to spend on the fun stuff.

**Outlet Stores**   Many people drive miles to outlet villages to snap up clearance bargains, which is fair enough. But now, lots of high street and high-end stores have online outlet stores, either via eBay or special websites, and you can actually check out the things you want without having to spend on traveling. Do remember though that just like a physical store, online stores are set out with your psychology in mind, and you may have to scroll through (instead of walk past) lots of other tempting looking offers to get to what you want!

So just as for necessary spending, when you're looking for something that's an option (even if you really want it), it's a good move to check more than one site to be sure you're getting a competitive deal.

Also online, don't forget about postage and packaging costs for delivery and for returns. If you're in store, you can pick it up, but some online outlets do charge you what seems a disproportionate amount for getting your purchases to you.

Another way you can save on shopping and eating out is through online discount vouchers. Many shops and restaurants offer coupons you can either redeem online or print off to take in person. There are also websites that pool together vouchers and coupons from a variety of companies, keeping you up to date with weekly e-mail alerts. Some restaurant chains also offer vouchers if you sign up to their site. That can be a pain with constant e-mails, but if you are going to eat there regularly anyway, it can save you money.

Cashback sites that reward you for shopping with shops and chains are another way to save money on your shopping. Just by clicking through to a site and making a purchase, you'll receive some money back for your efforts. However, just because there's cashback involved doesn't mean you won't find a cheaper deal elsewhere, so still shop around first, and if you do want to buy whatever it is, go for the best deal for you overall.

Loyalty cards are used in many areas (including gas, clothing, and food) to encourage you to spend with a particular retailer. And if you shop often at the same store, they can be a good way to save money that you can use for other things that you want. But if you end up spending more than you need, they're not so useful.

Typical situations are that you get so many credits, or so much discount, if you spend a given amount in a given period. And people do find themselves spending "just a few dollars" to "make it up" to the total that they need to qualify. If it's what you would have spent, fine, but it can lead to you leaking lots of small amounts of money, so check what you're doing and consciously think about whether it's appropriate to spend the extra money, or buy the extra pair, in order to get a bigger discount.

## SUMMARY

You'll probably want to buy loads of things I haven't even mentioned, but you know the principles: "needs" versus "wants" and "opportunity cost." Keep those in mind, and you'll get good value for your money.

And, in closing, a real-life example of a "want" that worked out much better than expected! I wet shave. I could use an electric razor, but I just like the way a real blade feels. I've never used a cut-throat or had somebody professional shave me (like you read about in English novels from the 30s with the manservant shaving the master!). So for my birthday one year, my wife bought me a shave at Trumper, probably the most famous barber in the world. It wasn't necessary, it was an expense that we didn't need to have, it meant that we didn't have that money for something else, and it obviously didn't have any ongoing value (I still needed to shave again the next day!). But it was an experience, and I wouldn't have missed it for "stuff" worth 10 times the price.

## NOTES

1. Drazen Prelec and Duncan Simester, "Always Leave Home Without It: A Further Investigation of the Credit-Card Effect on Willingness to Pay," *Marketing Letters* 12:1 (2001): 5–12.

2. Stephanie Wilson, "The Effect of Music on Perceived Atmosphere and Purchase Intentions in a Restaurant," *Psychology of Music* 31:1 (2003): 93–112.

3. Maggie Zhang, "11 Psychological Tricks Restaurants Use To Make You Spend More Money," http://www.businessinsider.com/restaurant-menus-spend-more-money-2014-7#ixzz3CErZkyp3 (accessed March 9, 2014).

Chapter 7

# Borrowing, Credit, and Debt

This chapter covers several topics that are actually quite different, but you will begin to be exposed to pieces of them. Therefore, it makes sense to think about the whole, especially since some effects, often unintended, can affect your financial picture for a long time.

The tricky bit of this is that one of the common aspects involves math but stick with me here (I haven't steered you wrong yet, have I?). You may think that the math of money and finance is really complicated and that you'll never get the hang of it (which is exactly what some professionals want you to think!). That's not the case. If you have a reasonable idea of what you want and how you make decisions, which you do now, the math falls in place pretty easily. As Einstein said, "Do not worry about your difficulties in Mathematics. I can assure you mine are still greater."[1] So you are in good company!

It helps to know where you're trying to get to with any problem so let's think about an ideal situation to get an idea of what you're trying to achieve.

The ideal would be that if you need money, you could borrow it and it didn't cost anything. This might be where your parents chime in "this is what we feel like now!" Your time at college is a great opportunity to shift your practice if you have always worked on the assumption that your parents are infinite money machines. You can become self-sufficient here and develop your own style.

You would have to pay the money back at some point, but it would be great if you could have the use of the money without having to pay anything for it. And, if your lender took responsibility for sorting out any problems that arose in the purchase (store didn't deliver, goods were inferior, and so on), that would be even better! Finally, the ideal would be that you could use the borrowed money as you liked and pay it back as you could.

That's what would be great. But you know it doesn't work that way—because of "risk" and "responsibility." (Remember, this is about living your values, and if you have gotten this far, I'm guessing that respect and independence are two of your values!) So let's look at how things are structured now.

## LENDERS

People lending money, or allowing you to use their money (give you credit), are usually in business. Even National and State Governments that may give you loans are run to an extent like businesses. And businesses want two things if they lend you money.

They want to know they will get their money back, so they want something that shows how you'll pay them back as well as promising something you own so that they can sell it to get their money if you can't pay them back. And they want their money to work for them even as it is being used by you. And because there is always a risk that you won't pay them back, they want you to pay them for that risk—more than if they just put the money in a bank and got paid some interest safely without having to take any trouble lending to you.

So people lending you money are going to want to have some security, something they can sell to get their money back if you can't pay them. It doesn't really matter, in business terms, *why* you can't pay them back— you can't get a job, you've had an accident and can't work (or are dead!), or if you have spent all the money and have no intention of paying them back—they just want to be able to get the money back. That's why if you get a car loan, the finance company will probably want the pink slip; when you buy a house, the lender holds the house deeds; and so on. They are trying to get some security that is worth at least as much as they are lending you. And with big loans, they may want you to take out insurance so that if something happens to you, they can get their money back more quickly. What we're talking about here is secured loans: You borrow money to buy something of value and the lender secures the loan with the item you bought, just in case you can't pay the money back.

You can get loans and credit without security—oddly enough, these are called "unsecured loans" (!)—and they tend to be shorter term. Credit cards work like that, so do most education loans. But think about this from the lenders business point of view. They are lending money, and they don't have a guarantee they'll get the money back—so if for any reason at all, you can't or won't pay them, they've lost their money. For taking the risk of lending without security (something to sell), the lender will charge a higher rate of interest.

So an underlying principle of loans, credit and (as we'll see) debt, is around interest rate:

### Interest Rates

This is where there's a bit of math. You probably know all this anyway, but I promised I'd make it really simple to make sure that even if you're totally math phobic you can follow it. So if it looks like I'm treating you like a child, I'm sorry but maybe you can use it to explain things simply to a friend or relative who is still mystified by it and thinks that finance is really complicated.

Interest rates are measured in percent, which is indicated by the symbol %. Percent is Latin for, "for each hundred." So 10 percent is 10 for each hundred, 55 percent is 55 for each hundred, and so on.

Imagine you've got $100 that you don't need for a year.

You invest it and you are promised five percent. What do you end up with at the end of the year?

You've got $100 and you're getting "five per hundred." You can probably work that out in your head as getting an extra $5, so you'd end up with $105. What you'd do if the figures were a bit more complicated is to multiply the $100 by 1.05 and you'd get the same thing.

The reason it's 1.05 is that our number system is based around 10s, and the way it is written means that the numbers after the decimal point are arranged in per 10 and per 100. For example, 0.55 is 5 per 10 plus 5 per 100, or you could say it as 55 per 100. As we want 5 percent, which we said was "5 for each 100," we want 0.05 because that is "none per 10, plus 5 per 100."

It's actually more complicated to write down than it is to do—you just multiply the amount of money you invest or borrow, by the interest rate expressed as a decimal (0.05, for example) and that's what you have (or owe) at the end of the year.

Which is great if you only invest or borrow for one year, and the interest rate is quoted for a year (not a month, or quarter, or week).

So what happens if you invest or borrow for a longer period?

Imagine you borrow $100 at 5 percent for 3 years. You can't just multiply the one year figure by three, because it's "compound" interest. Translation: The interest after one year is added to the $100 and the interest in the second year is calculated on the new total; it's "compounded" together. Are you noticing that the "math" we're doing is adding, multiplying, and dividing? You learned it in fourth grade—no worries!

You borrow $100. The interest rate is 5 percent, so as we just worked out, at the end of the first year, you'd owe $105. In the second year, you are again going to pay 5 percent, but because it is "compounded," you actually pay "5 per 100" of your money plus the interest so far. You've got $105, and you add "5 per 100" of the $105. So you multiply your $105 by 1.05 again, and you get $110.25, which is what you owe at the end of the second year. And for the third year, you multiply that by 1.05 again, which is $110.25 times 1.05, which is $115.76 (plus some fractions of a penny that we'll round down) and that is the amount you owe at the end of three years.

That really is all there is to it. You can use the calculator on your phone to do it or a spreadsheet or financial calculator, just to shortcut. What we get is that if somebody is going to lend you money, they're going to charge you interest on it, they're going to want more interest if they don't have any security (like a car or a house) that they can sell if you don't pay them, and they want their money back at whatever date you said you would pay it back.

And that means that the essential points are what interest rate you'll be charged, in what periods (monthly? quarterly? annually?) for how long, and how will you pay it back (monthly? quarterly? annually?).

Which brings us to:

**The Compound Interest Blind Spot**    Albert Einstein was once asked what was the most powerful force in the universe; he said, "compound interest."[2]

We'll look at an example with pizza, but move to student loans because it's not such a big leap from pizza (really). Imagine you want $10 to buy a pizza. You don't have $10, so you borrow it. You have two potential lenders. The first is a student loan company. They are geared up to longer term loans; they've got official backing, so they have a cushion if you don't pay them back. They charge you six percent.

Let's assume that $10 for the pizza goes onto your loan and you pay it back after 20 years (that sounds a long time, but it's certainly not the highest and it's fairly typical). You'll actually pay back $30.21 for that $10 pizza.

Remember, that's at an interest rate lower than you'll usually get even from an official loan that is meant to be beneficial to you. It means that you have to pay over *three times* as much as you borrowed for something you consumed in 1/2 hour (or less!). Compare it to what the banks would charge you (likely to be around 8%, if they get security; more if they don't) or a credit card (where the rates may be above 20%; remember, you are borrowing cash without security) and work out how much that pizza would then cost you. Moving right over to student loans, you can see why you may find that if you've borrowed, say, $10,000 over 4 years of college, you are going to take 15 or 20 years to pay it back, because you end up paying back 20 or 30 thousand dollars including the interest. Of course, unlike the pizza, the student loan gives you the education foundation for your job success, but it's worth knowing what your obligation will be when you graduate so you can realistically match your earning power and your debt.

That's the sort of thing Einstein meant about the power of compound interest.

There is another loan option, and it's one that a lot of people get fooled into taking because it seems more attractive. That option is a company that advertises short-term loans, often called a "payday loan" company. They don't tend to quote annual rates like 5 percent or 10 percent. They usually offer smaller amounts (usually a few hundred dollars rather than big amounts to cover a whole year) and say you can pay them back from next month's (or week's) allowance, pay, or whatever. Hence the term, *payday loan.* And the offers tend to be along the lines of "borrow $100 now and pay back just $125 next month," which, to most people, sounds OK—it's just $25, right?

So let's go back to pizza: You borrow your $10 for pizza on those terms and say you'll pay back $12.50 (the math is $10 + [$10 × 0.25]) next month. That doesn't sound too bad; it's "only" $2.50 extra, surely that won't cause a problem. But what if next month, you're short? You were short this time; you had to have some food and needed to borrow. Why would you have enough cash next month not only to buy this month's pizza but last months (and the interest) too? They agree to let you extend the loan, but you're paying interest on the interest (it's com-pounded, remember). So at the end of 2 months, you owe $15.63, and if that gets tricky (you had to borrow $10 for pizza; how are you suddenly going to find $15.63 to buy nothing at all?), the amount after 3 months is $19.53. Your debt sails past the 3 times the amount a lower rate loan would be over 20 years in the 5th month; by 6 months, you owe $38.15 (I rounded the fractions of a cent down; a loan company probably won't do that for you). If you did wait until after you graduated to pay the $10 back (just 4 years, not 20), you'd have to pay back $448,415 (I've let you off the odd cents again), just under a cool half million!

I normally don't like scaring people, but I hope that terrifies you as much as it does me.

One reason it scares me is that I've seen clients with debts like that, whom I can't constructively help with advice, that really did get into trouble over small amounts that they genuinely thought they would easily pay back.

Despite all the warnings, the authority of somebody like Einstein, and although the math is pretty simple, many people continue to have trouble with loans, debts, credit cards, and so on. So, consider this: Would you rather have your money working for you or for someone else? If the answer is "someone else," then payday lending is for you. If it's "for me," then before you take a loan, consider your benefit: A pizza is pretty short term; do you have another choice that you don't need a loan for?

I've talked a lot about your brain, and here's a good place to come back to it: Another reason people have trouble is something called optimism bias. You might have looked at the figures above and maybe even done some cal-culations yourself and thought, "I won't get into that position, I'll make sure I can pay loans back." And that's a good, responsible attitude. But human brains have this optimism bias; we expect that the future will work out for us. (If you're interested, you can look it up there is at least one really good book about the research, why we are like that and how it operates), but basically we evolved to be hopeful, to feel we can cope.

That's another reason why I emphasized the situation of people like Art, who found he suddenly didn't have the money he thought he'd have because a few dollars slipped away here and there. Imagine if he hadn't realized what was going on and had borrowed to cover the shortfall. After a semester of spending maybe $100 a month more than he meant to, and borrowing to cover it, he'd not be down $400, he'd be down over $1,000, with the interest mounting each week until his entire income wouldn't cover the interest, let alone paying back any of the loan itself.

Loans are important for large purchases, a house or an education, for example. The piece that I want you to take away here is where we started this conversation: Know why you are going to school. If you have that figured out, then you will make a choice for financing your goal that works for you. And make sure you've worked through the previous chapters, how much are you going to need; you don't want to arrange a student loan on a (relatively) low rate and be confident of paying it off soon after you graduate, only to have to take out short-term, expensive loans that ruin all your calculations (and peace of mind) because you forgot things that you needed to pay for.

And if you are, like Terri whom we met in Chapter 1, keen to go on to graduate school, think about how that's going to work and do the math on the potential of return, and payback, over time. The theme is the same as throughout the book: Make a choice that works for you and develop a plan that can work within your needs and constraints. There was a news spot a month or two before I wrote this about a women with over $100,000 in student loan debt—her graduate degrees were in Latin. That's an interesting subject, and having studied it for a couple of years, I find it useful for both English and some European languages, but common sense —and a scan of job postings and "highest paying professions"—will probably tell you that it's going to be a *very* long time before those loans will be paid back, even if they are at a really low rate of interest. Lending institutions will not have a conversation about your goals and values, but that's why you picked up this book and have read this far, isn't it? My goal for you is to help you make sure that if you end up like that woman, you do it from choice, not by accident, and you go in with your eyes open. It's to allow you to have that mark of maturity, being responsible for your own decisions and the outcomes and not being dependent on other people (your parents, a lending institution, or whoever) to take the responsibility for you, and to assemble the support team that can help you do just that.

**Comparing Rates** As we've seen, it's important to work out how to pay loans off as soon as possible—if you have to have them at all, of course! The effect of leaving a debt unpaid and the interest rolling up for longer than you need ought to give you nightmares.

But the other thing that makes a big difference is the interest rate: If you do have to borrow, you want to have to pay the lowest interest rate you can.

There is a standard measure of the interest rate that takes into account how often the interest "accrues" (how often it's added, whether it's daily, weekly, monthly, quarterly, or yearly). It also has to take into account charges (such as fees for the loan, penalties for not meeting payments, early redemption charges—if you pay off early, some loans have penalties!). It's called Effective Annual Percentage Rate (EAPR).

EAPR is designed to give people a good idea of what they'll actually be paying with each loan, irrespective of what the charges are called (administration charge, arrangement fee, and so on), how often the interest accrues, the term, and other details. And sometimes it's hard to figure out just what that rate is, but keep asking the question until you get the answer—remember, you are the one paying to rent their money!

The problem is mainly with the compounding effect that we talked about. If you look at the interest rates that are usually given in adverts (often called the "headline" rate or "nominal rate"), you might see a figure such as 7 percent. It might look as if it makes no difference whether that is 7 percent a year or 7/12 percent each month; after all, if you have 7/12 each month, it adds up to 7 in a year, so it's the same, isn't it?

No, it's very different.

You know the story of the early Dutch settlers in the United States who bought the island of Manhattan from the Native Americans for the equivalent of 60 Guilders (about $40 at the time) in trade goods. Imagine they'd borrowed that $40. Compound interest at 7 percent annually would mean they'd owe about 7 trillion dollars (7 with 12 zeros after it) today! Looking at real estate sites, the whole of Manhattan real estate today appears to be worth about 8 trillion dollars. But if they'd borrowed the money at 7 percent accrued monthly (7/12% each month), they'd now owe about 16 trillion dollars—they would owe more than twice as much as all the real estate in Manhattan put together!

So you want the *Effective* APR (EAPR) because that includes the effect of compounding other than annually.

In many countries, including the United States of America, lenders for certain loans (mortgages for houses, for example) have to quote a rate, the Annual Percentage Rate (APR). In some countries, the APR and the EAPR are pretty much the same thing—what you're quoted is what you pay. The trouble is, that in general, what is quoted as the APR in the United States is expressed as the periodic interest rate times the number of compounding periods in a year, which is the nominal interest rate rather than the effective one. However, the APR must include certain noninterest charges and fees, so it does give you more information than simply believing the advertised rate.

The calculation and disclosure of APR are covered in the Truth in Lending Act. The rules apply particularly with mortgages, but there are also rules regarding credit cards and other types of credit; if you want to look up some of the details about the rules, they're on the Federal Deposit Insurance Corporation (FDIC) site.

So you can get some information, but not always everything you need, by law.

If you're getting a loan, ask for the APR at least (preferably get the EAPR). If the lender won't give you the APR, for example, saying that it isn't appropriate because it's not a loan that runs for a year (a common dodge with payday loan companies and the like), walk away. If the lender won't give you the information, there's only one reason: The benefit of the loan is to the lender, not to you.

As an example of what they'd tell you if they were working in your favor, the EAPR on that loan of $100 to pay back $125 next month (or $10 for $12.5) is 1,355 percent! Think that's bad? There was a loan company offering short-term loans at one percent a day. That's 261,900 percent EAPR!

See what I mean. If someone said to you, "I'll lend you money if you pay me interest at over 1,000 percent" (let alone over 100,000%), you'd probably think they were mad, or joking. But people take out those loans every day (that's why there are so many of those companies around; it's a very profitable business to be in). The people who take the loans aren't stupid; they just aren't aware of what decisions they are making; they don't realize that they're biased toward believing that they can pay it off because it "doesn't sound like much."

So be careful about loans, think through how much you really need them, consider when you'll realistically be able to pay them back (it probably won't be short term), and make sure you know the real rate you'll pay, the EAPR. Then, if you have to borrow, keep the loan as low as possible, take the lowest rate you can find, with a reputable lender, and if you can do without it, do.

**Credit Cards** These can be really useful, but they take careful handling. Put simply, they work by you having a card with a preset loan limit (a credit limit). Every month (usually) you get a bill and have about 14 days to pay it. If you pay it in full, you don't get charged interest (some cards have an annual fee that you have to pay anyway; some don't). If you don't pay it off in full, you have to pay interest on the outstanding amount, usually from the date you spent the money (not from the date of the bill). The EAPR is invariably up above 20 percent even when base interest rates—the ones that banks pay to one another—are about 1 percent. So they're expensive if you have to pay anything at all. And if you miss a payment (you forget, or don't have the money), you get extra charges as well, which can easily push the EAPR up to 50 percent or more. The amount outstanding (including the interest) counts against your credit limit. So if you have a limit of, say, $3,000 and you have $1,000 outstanding, you've only got another $2,000 to use, then the card will be blocked and you can't use it until you've taken the outstanding amount down. That's what people mean when they say the card is "maxed out."

But credit is good, right? Yes, if it is your credit: Credit cards are called that because they show up on a bank's credit ledger, not yours! It is helpful to think of a credit card transaction as a loan and match the useful period to the loan. A washing machine will last longer than dinner, so you might justify rolling the washing machine purchase over for a few month. But dinner? When you don't see the cash going out of your wallet, it's easier to spend with the intention to pay the card off. But it can be a downward cycle to get into. Just imagine: if you roll over the washing machine purchase, and then you need to fix the car (which will also serve you for several years—provided the transmission is fixed), and so on? You can finish up convincing yourself that rolling up the debts is worthwhile—which it might be, for each loan in isolation but taken altogether the loans get out of hand.

Again, sorry to be scary, but that's what happens when people, with good intentions, get optimistic, fail to understand the power of compound interest, and start to think that the answer to a problem with debt is more debt. And, yes, that sounds stupid; you'd think anybody would know that borrowing your way out of a debt problem is a bad idea, but millions of people do it, and so do many countries! Everybody can give you a good reason: Nationally, it's, "we're stimulating the economy"; personally it's "to tide me over until . . . .," but the fact is, it's almost certain to result in a disaster for an individual (and it's not usually too effective for a country either).

So treat a credit card like any other form of debt; you don't want to be in a position where you can't pay it off and be paying huge rates of interest and possibly additional charges.

Store cards are basically a type of credit card, but, as the name suggests, set up by a store rather than directly by a bank (they're usually actually run by a bank and promoted by the store). I mentioned before that things like loyalty cards can be useful, as long as you don't get carried away and buy things over your budget to get the next discount or something. You can treat store credit cards the same way that you treat other types of credit cards (with extreme caution, as I'll explain). But sometimes there is a combined store loyalty and credit card—so what do you do if you like the store and use it a lot? It's your decision; read through the rest of the chapter and think about it—but generally I'd advise most people to steer clear of store credit cards. The rates are often even higher, and you will likely start getting daily e-mails offering "special deals" or "double points" or "insider sales." Consider them carefully. You might be able to use it to your advantage, but be very, very careful if you think you can—the optimism bias makes us all think we're the exception that won't end up losing money but making it, and even if you think you're a good gambler, the odds are very much against you!

These days, you don't need to carry much cash, and you can apply for unlimited cards (oddly, your credit score can improve when you add cards). But I'd suggest you limit both the number and type of credit cards you have; they can be really handy in an emergency, but the human brain works in certain ways and one of them is to represent some money—money on credit, money you find in the street, or that you win in a lottery for example—as being less valuable than other money—that you worked for hours at really unpleasant jobs to earn, for example. It's something called "mental accounting" and it's part of us. The way to deal with it is to accept that you're a human being and that you will have that sort of bias. You want to learn to allow for your tendency to treat credit as being like money in a game like second life, rather than real. You can use mental accounting and other mental foibles to your advantage (because you can, they're brilliant tools if you use them right)—more on that in a later chapter. But for credit cards, the thing to remember is that you will almost certainly be tempted to spend more with them.

So think about it. You know yourself. You know how good you are at avoiding impulse spending, controlling yourself, stepping back to think about decisions before acting. And if you don't know because you haven't had much experience, experiment in small ways. If you know you are a spender, pay for everything with cash and keep a card (like American Express) that has to be paid off (there isn't a rollover period) for emergencies! Remember the money story exercise in Chapter 2? Revisit your story; now may be the perfect time to rewrite it by trying something new, a card with a small limit that you only use for clothes, for example. Just because you've always been one way or believed one thing in the past, there's nothing stopping you changing in future.

If you keep track of what you're spending and know how much you've got (and aren't like Art and have money slipping away and not know where it's gone), then you might think about having a debit card. Debit cards are similar to a credit card, but with a very important difference. They are linked to your bank account. You can "sign for" or enter a PIN (Permanent or Personal Identity Number, basically a security system to make sure it's you using the card), and the money is debited to your account, very like writing a check. The difference between that and a credit card is that you don't have any credit limit; if you don't have the money in the account, the card won't work. So rather than give you a pre-agreed credit (credit card), it debits the money to your actual account (debit card).

If you want to try out having a credit card, without so much risk of getting into debt, a debit card can be useful. It's not entirely risk free though. You can still spend money in your account that was intended for spending on important things later in the month—and you can spend it all today on something that really you don't need.

So even with a debit card (and certainly with a credit card), you have to be even more careful than you should always be with cash and bear in mind your opportunity cost of spending on whatever you want at the moment.

Credit cards, in themselves, are not dangerous; they are easy, convenient, and certainly have improved money flow (I'm old enough to remember how hard it was to travel without credit cards!). But they don't run out, like money does, so you can continue to buy well beyond your ability to pay. So this is where you come in: You get to choose! Ask yourself seriously "why do I want this card, is it really going to be so useful to me that it's worth running the risks of getting debts that I will have trouble handling? And, hand on heart, am I confident that I can control myself if I see a pair of shoes/gadget/video game/music download (delete where applicable) that I want but don't have the money to buy?"

If you are absolutely certain you can cope, and perhaps have tried yourself out with a debit card for a few months or a year, there are three good reasons for having a card if you can use it wisely.

One is that it can be convenient, you don't have to carry so much cash (although you can get the same effect with a debit card, with less risk), and they are more acceptable in more places—some won't take debit cards (probably because they want to encourage reckless spending!).

Another, is that you can, if you are very careful, get some free credit, but only even think about this if you are really disciplined and know that you can stick to the plan, always save the money to pay off the bill (not spend it on something else in the meantime), and will have the organization to time it right. I do this sort of thing, but I've had a lot of practice and I've got bank arrangements set up to make sure the bill is paid each month even if I'm away or I forget—it makes a small profit each year, but it does take a lot of organizing.

The other, and probably the only really good reason to have a credit card, is that it usually offers you more protection if you buy something.

Credit cards offer the most protection—as long as the item or service you bought cost over $100, you can claim against your card provider under Section 75 of the Consumer Credit Act to get your money back. Be sure to check about specific cards; the coverage varies with the card.

## MAKING DECISIONS

What we've covered so far in this chapter is making the best decision for you on credit, debt, and connected issues. It's wise to think through what you really want (Chapter 1), what you are like and how you think (Chapter 2), and how you're planning to get to where you want from where you are (Chapter 3). The idea is that you can think these things through in advance, decide what you can afford, and what (if any) debt or credit you need and can handle. Then you can plan how you're going to deal with it. This bolsters your money practice by adding things to help you get what you want, rather than set yourself up to fail by exposing yourself to temptation and hoping for the best—because giving in to temptation is just easier sometimes, even if the outcome isn't the best!

I'll give you a short list of potential loan, banking, and credit expenses. But first, there's another aspect of handling money that is important.

### Security

No doubt about it, we live in an online world, and you probably don't think twice about tweets, Instagrams, and all the other electronic communicating you do. But there are people on the Internet working just as hard to gather your information as you may be to protect it. So a few words on protecting your identity and your information:

- Develop strong passwords. Make them 8 characters or longer—the more characters, the more permutations, so the harder it is to work out or guess. Use numbers, symbols, and a mix of capital and lower case letters. You can use substitutions like $ or 5 for s (use symbols that look like the letter); an example on the Microsoft site being ILuv2PlayB@dm1nt()n (which hopefully you can read and potentially remember, but wouldn't guess even if you knew the person liked badminton!).

- Use a password keeper (there are several reviews and recommendations on CNET.com and PCMagazine.com).
- Keep your social security number safe.
- Check your credit monthly (www.creditkarma.com is a free and useful site).
- Review your credit card statements, bills, bank statements (it's too easy just to pay the amount that comes across in automatic billing; make sure all the charges are yours).

Have the latest antimalware software; ensure your firewall is sound and all your devices are both synched and protected. You can contact the college IT department as to what they recommend and whether they offer free software and/or security assistance. Remember, on campus you are using at best a semipublic network, so it's best to make sure all your money (and your other data) is as safe as you can make it.

## Costs of Credit

I've tried to make sure you're aware of the pros and cons of having loans, credit cards, and so on. You have to make the decisions and choose whether you have debts or not. But you'll almost certainly have some costs, if only for a bank account.

So here's a list of potential costs—make sure you build this into your budget; it ensures you don't have any unpleasant surprises. It also allows you to check the latest position. If the cost for credit is more than you've budgeted for, it's a cue to look at what's going on, what payment had you forgotten, what is costing you more than you expected? You can then sort things out before it becomes a real problem.

- Bank account charges
- Overdraft fees and interest. I didn't say much about this, because unauthorized overdrafts (where you don't agree a limit with the bank beforehand) are always at crippling interest, and authorized ones (where you agree with them) are probably better sorted out as a loan.
- Car or other long-term loan payments
- Credit card payments

## SUMMARY

Compare prices, for everything from cheese to loans, and make sure you are comparing on the same basis (ideally the EAPR for loans).

Compound interest is your friend when you are saving and investing but can dig you into a hole fast if you are spending using loans. So think about your opportunity cost, the life of the item you are buying, and the usefulness of that item as you consider whether, and how, to make it yours.

Make sure you know what interest rate you'll be charged, in what periods (monthly? quarterly? annually?) for how long, and how you will pay it back (monthly? annually? quarterly?).

Credit cards can be useful in emergencies (e.g., while traveling, if something happens) or for large purchases. But do note: If you can't afford something without a credit card, if you don't have the money set aside, then buying on credit will leave you in a hole and limit your choices and your opportunities.

Secure your online financial activity by securing all of your online activity (including the equipment you use).

And, above all, remember that financial math is what you learned in fourth grade—add, subtract, divide—and if something seems "too good to be true," it usually is.

## NOTES

1. Albert Einstein, "Don't worry about your difficulties with mathematics," http://www.brainyquote.com/quotes/quotes/a/alberteins125370.html (accessed September 4, 2014).

2. Albert Einstein, "The most powerful force in the universe," http://www.brainyquote.com/quotes/quotes/m/mignonmcla158995.html (accessed September 4, 2014).

Chapter 8

# Saving and Investing

Investing is probably what you think of when you hear the words "financial planning." Traders on Wall Street yelling at one another in a dealing room that resembles a well-dressed mosh pit at a rock concert and men with perma-tans and extensive cosmetic surgery hissing "get me my broker" into an intercom. Right?

I expect those things go on, but the reality today is more like what Michael Lewis describes in his book *Flash Boys*. And I'm sure you've heard a lot of advertising recently telling you that "you ought to start saving when you're young," and "a dollar saved is a dollar earned"—which are respectively so obvious as to be useless and not really helpful in guiding you to your goals!

In Chapter 2 we talked about your money story, which is where you are with how you think about money. In this chapter, I'm going to introduce you to a tool that will help you rewrite your money story and bring it up to date—to get you where you'd like to go.

First, some terms. When I mention savings, I mean money not earmarked for the "needs" (food, clothing, housing, transportation) you have. Rather, saving is when you take some of the money you could spend on "wants" (entertainment, travel), and you deliberately put it away in a savings account.

Investing, in my terms, is where you are looking longer term, certainly over a year and perhaps more. It's where you are trying to get that money to grow for the future rather than spend it today or over the next year.

And it can get confusing, because you have to save, to put the money aside, in order to be able to invest; if you have nothing saved, you've got nothing that isn't being spent that you can invest. In sum, *saving* is about putting money aside, taking it out of your usual spending pattern, while *investing* is putting the money to work to grow for the longer term. So, really, investing is a subset of savings.

There are a few other terms we need to define as well. When we talk about investing specifically, there are five things that are useful to know in order to help make the best decisions for you. There are *rate of return*, *risk*, *time*, *liquidity*, and *amount*. I'll say a bit about each of these in turn, and then we'll look at what you might want to achieve to see how these five things affect your decisions.

## RATE OF RETURN

We talked about rate of interest in the last chapter. The difference between rate of interest and rate of return is that rather than you paying it out to borrow money, rate of return is paid to you. It can come in the form of interest or dividend income on stock, coupon income on bonds, or rental income from property. It could even include something like capital appreciation (if something increases in value, the annual rate of increase is effectively an additional return to any income). The concept is the same as rate of interest, but in all of the cases above, the rate of return is what comes back to you from the entity that is using your money.

Sometimes you will know with certainty what the rate of return will be. With banks or Government bonds, Treasury Bonds, for example, the rate of return is specifically quoted ("the current yield on the 30 year bond is 3.15%"). In this case, interest and rate of return are synonyms. Other times, it's not certain at all—"anticipated returns" or "previous figures suggest returns of . . . ." A *guaranteed* return is pretty much that; it's going to take some strange situations for the guarantee not to be honored—but always check it. If it doesn't say guaranteed, check it out especially carefully because you might find that the figure you were given was only a guess, and the reality may be very different!

Now, this may seem like a side trip, but bear with me. Two things are important when you are looking at returns over time. One is inflation, and the other is required rate of return. We live in a world where we have inflation, which simply means that an amount of money gets less valuable as time goes on. I'm sure you've heard adults in your life say things like "Boy, things are more expensive today than they were when I was young." or "When I was young, movies were only 10 cents." or "I can remember when a gallon of gas cost less than $1.00!" (if that was in 1979, in today's money, the cost is $3.16—that's inflation). The point is, if inflation is running at 5 percent (so money is effectively going down in value by 5% a year in terms of what it will actually buy you), then a return of 6 percent is worth only 1 percent in *real* terms.

The other element of return that is important, in fact I'd say is more important than anything else, is your required rate of return. Required rate is not talked about a lot, because the balance in the advisor/client relationship today is tipped toward the advisor. The required rate of return, put simply, is what you require (no kidding!) to get what you want. So if you want to have, say, enough money to cover your postgrad studies in 4 years, and that will be $10,000, and you've been given $10,000 by a relative, your required rate of return is 0—you already have the money, you don't need it to grow. You may think "I can't just let it sit there" or someone may say to you, "you should be making that money work for you." Well, here's the thing: You've achieved the goal of saving for postgraduate studies, so protect that goal and move to another—don't get distracted by "should."

On the other hand, if you have $1,000, and you need the same $10,000 in 4 years, you need $9,000 from your $1,000, which means your required rate is about 78 percent compound each year. A really good advisor would tell you that a 78-percent return on your money is highly uncertain.

So, in the first case, your required rate of return is 0. In the second, it is 78 percent. In the first case, you can use your money as a tool; in the second case, your 78-percent required rate of return will most likely end up using *you*; as you nervously check your account to see your gain—or loss. Does it make sense to you to have that anxiety in the first case as well, when you don't need to? You've got enough to worry about getting through these next four years.

## RISK

It is important to define the word "risk" in talking about investments. The dictionary definition of "risk" is "the potential of losing something of value, weighed against the potential to gain something of value." In investing theory, you can put a mathematical value on *risk* because, basically, you know the odds of it happening and how much it will cost if it happens. If you can't put numbers on it so you have to estimate or guess the figures, it's not risk, it's *uncertainty*. There are some good books, about how unpredictable life is, that go into "nonlinear dynamics," chaos theory, complexity, and so on—they are fascinating subjects (if you're interested, Google those terms). But here's a simple explanation of what I mean.

Imagine that you want to get a big return on your money, say that 78 percent that I mentioned. You want to control your investment risk, to be able to give yourself the best chance of controlling your return and getting what you need. You decide there are three options (I know there are loads more, but bear with me!), and you have $1,000. You can go to Vegas and play roulette or blackjack, you can go to Saratoga and play the horses, or you can go to a broker and invest in business. What do you know about them? Well, in Vegas, you know how many slots there are in the roulette wheel, how many win for you, what you get if you win. You know what you lose if you lose—$1,000. You know that when the wheel stops you'll get paid or lose your stake. You know that once the wheel starts to spin they won't change the bets or the wheel, or introduce another ball. With blackjack, you know how many cards there are, when you've won or lost, which combinations win, and so on (to the point that the casino will get upset if they see you card counting, because it means they think you've got too much control over your risk). At Saratoga, you know most of the things, you know what your bet is ($1,000), you know what you win if you win because the payout on each horse is published before the race. In fact, the only thing you don't know is what the odds of the horse winning are. All of these things (except the chance of a horse winning) are risks; you know what the odds are, you know the payoff, you know what and when you win or lose, and you know the rules don't change part way through.

Now consider a business. Do you know what you "win?" No, it might do fantastically well or it might fail completely and nobody knows what the odds are of either happening (they can make educated guesses, but nobody knows; in the same way as nobody knows the odds of a particular horse winning), and nobody knows how much that would pay you or whether you'd lose everything (or more, or less) if it all goes wrong. Do you know when you get paid for your "win," if you do? No, business goes on; it doesn't stop at the end of the day and pay you. Do you know the rules won't change? No, somebody might come along tomorrow with new technology that puts the business you've invested in out of business. That's all uncertainty; none of it is risk, you can't actually put quantities on any of it for certain, you can only guess.

So tell me, which is a "gamble" and which is a "calculated risk?"

I'm not for a moment suggesting that a casino or a racetrack is a good investment! You can be absolutely certain about the risk, and that certainty is that you will lose money—that's why bookmakers and casino owners are so rich; nobody ever, ever, beats the house long term. But it is absolutely mathematically predictable; you can calculate the risk, you will lose, but you'll lose in a very predictable way. With business, you cannot predict—people will tell you they are certain about particular investments, but they can't be—in real life we simply cannot be that sure.

So when you hear people talk about "risk assessment" for investments, remember that what they are talking about is a guess. Calling something a risk doesn't make it less uncertain; it just suggests that whoever is calling it a risk either doesn't know or has forgotten that they're assuming they can predict something mathematically that is actually impossible to predict in any way at all, including mathematically.

There's a corollary to this. Nothing is "risk free." Nobody knows exactly what is going to happen, so even things that are really unlikely (say, Martian invasion or a lottery win) can't be entirely ruled out. If you read up on chaos and complexity theory, it does tend to make you realize that when people selling investment products or services talk about accurately measuring your "risk attitude" and how they "match the investment risk to your profile," and so on, they are actually exposing their extreme ignorance of reality.

If you are investing, however, it is very important for you to consider how conservative or aggressive you are. You can be conservative (want to protect your investment at all costs), aggressive (can take some ups and downs), or somewhere in between. You will hear the term "risk tolerance" used by advisors to mean "investing comfort level." I could have a whole chapter on this subject, but for now, be aware of your comfort level before you invest. I knew a doctor once who, early in his career, invested in the stock of a company he was sure was going to be a winner because of the drug it produced. He watched the stock every day and got so anxious about losing money when the stock went down that he sold his shares: It was a good lesson for him in recognizing his comfort level with investing and the prospect that shares could go down as easily as go up.

## TIME

We covered a bit of this in the last chapter. It's about the power of compound interest. If you've got a situation where you're getting income (whether it is interest as such or dividends, coupon, and so on) and you let it "roll up," you get that compounding effect—you start to get interest on the interest. As we saw with you paying to a lender, over one year (or month, if interest is monthly, and so on), there is no difference between "simple" interest and compound. But as soon as it rolls up multiple times, the compounding effect takes over and the money that's compounded (whether you owe it, or receive it) grows faster. And the rate increases with the compounding effect.

Let's take an example. Say you have that $1,000 we mentioned above. You can obviously buy $1,000 worth of things now, and that would be nice. If you can save it, put it on one side, and get 5 percent (in a bank account, for the sake of example), after a year you'd have $1,050. Nice, but not a huge return. Imagine you can leave it to roll up for the four years you're in college. Even at the same rate of 5 percent, it is worth $1,215.51. Again, nice, if you'd had 4 years of earning $50 of simple interest, you'd have only made $200 to add to your $1,000; the extra $15.51 ($1,215.51–$1,200) is the compounding effect over time.

Say you go on and do a PhD taking another 4 years, and at the same 5 percent, you'd have $1,477.46—you're up $77.46 on what you'd get from the 1 year simple interest 8 times over.

If you can leave it longer still, it grows ever faster: After 16 years, you're up $382.86, and after 24 years, $1,225.10. Your gain increases more and more rapidly the longer you leave the money.

That's why I said at the start of the chapter that "start saving early" is so obvious as to be useless—once you realize how powerful compound interest is and how much impact time has on it, it's a no-brainer to start saving as early as possible. The challenge is finding money to save, which is why I've emphasized opportunity cost (there are always great things to spend money on right now) and why I defined saving as taking money from your "wants" bucket.

I had a client whose father told him, when he was a teen and started summer jobs, that a good habit to get into was to save 10 percent of everything he made. In his first summer job, he made $100 a week, and $10 didn't sound like much to save, while $10 a week would buy some things that he'd like right now. But he trusted his father (and the power of compound interest over time), saved the money, and then saw how it built up—and it became a habit that he uses to this day. It sounds tough, but if you're going to make the best decisions for *you*, you have to know what your choices are and be prepared to plan ahead for the things you really want.

## LIQUIDITY

This is about how accessible your money is to you. If you have a bank account and can withdraw money any time, then it is "totally liquid." If you have to give a month's notice to withdraw, your money is often described as "semiliquid." You may be able to get at the money before the month is up, but you usually get charged a fee for it. Property (a house, land, art, or jewelry) is a classic "illiquid" investment. You can't be sure that you'll be able to get the money quickly if you need it in a hurry. In fact, you may not be able to get your money back at all in certain market conditions.

The point is that generally, you would expect a higher return on something that is illiquid, and the harder it is to turn into cash, the higher return you'd expect. If you want to have the convenience and the safety net of being able to get at your money at a moment's notice, you will receive a lower return for that convenience.

And this is where "saving" and "investing" sometimes get confusing: You want savings to be available for emergencies so you need it liquid. If you're investing, you are deciding to put the money away for the longer term and you want it to grow, so you may be prepared to tie it up and not have it available, in return for it growing at a faster rate.

Often, you'll want a mix of liquid and illiquid. You may decide, however, that this isn't going to work for you at the moment. And that is why you are reading this book: to learn what works for you by assessing different options for the use of your money so it helps you do what you want to do.


## AMOUNT

The fifth thing that will affect your decisions in investing is the required amount. There are ways to reduce the minimum required for an investment, which we'll mention, but the basic point is there's usually a "floor level" for an investment—and it helps to focus on what the various costs of different options are.

So, now you have the five elements: *rate of return*, *risk*, *time*, *liquidity*, and *amount*, and I hope it's clear exactly why the book is structured the way it is. Imagine you want to have money available in six months for something that's really going to enhance your chances of getting your dream job when you graduate, and you have that money now. You want to put the money somewhere other than your mattress, so you go to a financial advisor to see what to do. And he tells you about something that has a great rate of return, a small investment on your part and minimal risk—without really finding out whether you have a plan or not. What you know is: You don't want to take *any* risk you don't have to take, you don't want to tie your money up at all not even part of it, and your time horizon is six months. What matters to you is avoiding any risk of not being able to do whatever it is in six months, and because you already have the money, your required rate of return is zero percent!

We started with what *you* wanted, what *you're* like, what plans *you* have to get where you want to go from where you are. And that's the point: You can calmly say "thank you for your time; this doesn't meet my needs."

If, on the other hand, there is something you don't have the money for, you still have the same priorities and questions for yourself; you just get a slightly different set of answers. Imagine there is something you want to do in a month and you can almost afford it. Out of the blue, you get an option to spend a year abroad in your third college year, which would be a really fantastic experience and look great on your résumé, and you'd need quite a lot more money for.

Where do you start deciding what to do: with rate of return? Or with questions like, what do I want, how much do I want it, what am I prepared to give up to get it? Maybe you decide that the year abroad is just impossible, so you go for your original one-month plan. Or maybe you decide that, if you save the money you would have spent in a month, put away some money from your part-time job, economize, negotiate hard with your relatives, and so on, you can get the year away if you get a return of X percent on your money. Great, you know what your required rate of return is. You know what your timescale is (two years), you know what liquidity you need (you're happy to tie the money up for two years). What you now want to do is to look at the expected rate of return and how much risk there is, and ideally get a guaranteed rate of return (and one that is "real," just in case the cost of the year away goes up with inflation) so you can make sure you get what you want.

The place to start is *you* and what you want your money to do for you, not with your money and what somebody else tells you is "best" for your money—because if you're thinking about what is best for your money, how much attention are you paying to what is best for you?


## TYPES OF INVESTMENT AND PLACES FOR SAVING

Basically, there are four types of investments and places for savings: cash deposits, bonds, shares, and property. There are many other things you can invest in: art, metals, derivatives (things like futures, options, and so on), racehorses; the list goes on. But until you've got a reasonable idea about the four main ones, looking at the variants is likely to be confusing (and potentially financially disastrous!).

Here's a summary of those types. As with rate of return, risk, and so on, I'm giving you the basics. If you're interested, there are plenty of books that give you everything you could possibly want to know about them.

## Cash Deposits

A "deposit" account means one that pays interest. (A standard checking account usually doesn't pay). Essentially, you are giving the company (usually a bank or a credit union) the use of your money, and they provide you with something in return. With a standard checking account, you get to write checks (or use a debit card) instead of having to carry large wads of cash everywhere, and you get various other services depending on the exact terms of the account. They might pay a tiny rate of interest, but that's pretty rare.

The general picture of a deposit account (sometimes called a CD or Certificate of Deposit) is one where you give them (a bank or financial institution, for example) the use of your money, and in return you get paid some interest each year, month, or whatever. If we look at our investment and savings variables, for an account the rate of return is usually pretty low, but the risk is also low. The risk isn't zero, everything in life carries risk, and banks and other financial institutions have been known to collapse—but it's rare and relatively, it's a safe place. In the United States, amounts up to $250,000 are insured by FDIC insurance, so, again, your risk is minimal. With amount, there are accounts you can open with a single dollar, and generally you can get at the money immediately, so it's liquid, which leaves time. Usually, the longer you leave the money with them, the higher rate of return you'll get. Consequently, the time, the liquidity, and the return are linked; the less access you have to the money in the short term, and the longer you're prepared to leave the money with them, the more you get paid.

Those are the essentials. You can probably work out that it's quite flexible. If you're saving (short term, put the money away), you can get an account that fits. You can open it with a few dollars (the required amount is small), you can have immediate access (liquid), you probably want it for something at the end of the semester or certainly within the year (term) then you can get it, it is very unlikely your money will disappear (risk), but you won't get much interest paid (rate of return). If you're looking longer term, perhaps to your senior year, you would look for an account that was for three years (term), that required six months' notice if you wanted to take the money back (semiliquid), but that paid you higher interest (rate of return). That might require you to put in more money, say $500 rather than $1 (amount), and it would be as relatively safe as the other account (risk).

## Bonds

Governments, National, state, or local, throughout the world often want to borrow money, as do companies. But their budgets are big (California, for instance, has a bigger budget than most countries). So when they borrow, they borrow a lot—millions, maybe billions of dollars over long periods for huge projects. And it makes sense to break the loan up into smaller pieces, usually called bonds, of, say, $1,000 each. That way, money comes from a range of sources, which may provide you with an investment opportunity. Imagine trying to get one company to float the loan for the Big Dig in Boston!

So, basically a bond is a loan to a Government (local, state, or federal) or a corporation that will pay interest (also called "the coupon"), and the Government or corporation pay back at some date in the future (called the redemption date).

Look at this in terms of our variables. There is generally a minimum *amount*. Bonds are tradable, so they are usually *liquid*. The *risk* is variable—Governments like the United States are pretty safe (they can go down, but if they do, it's likely that very little is going to be safe anyway), but some countries are not so stable (recently in the news, for example, Turkey and Greece) and are therefore more likely to default (not pay the money back). Similarly, some companies are pretty safe (not so much as a major, stable Government, but close to it); some are, frankly, quite unstable. Consequently, the *rate of return* can vary; you'd expect a higher return from a less stable country or organization than you would for US Treasury bonds. With time, theoretically you could get a bond that will be redeemed (meaning the company will repay the loan) in the short term so you could have a month or so. For example, if you buy a General Electric eight percent 2015 bond, it means you are buying a bond issued by General Electric that pays eight percent per year and comes due (is redeemed) in 2015, which means (at this writing) that you are buying a bond that only has one year left before it is redeemed. If, however, you buy a General Electric 6 percent 2044, you are buying a 30-year bond that will pay you 6 percent of the face value (which we assumed was $1,000). However, for various reasons (which you can look up if you're interested; try bond redemption and par price), you would usually look on them as investments for years rather than months.

### Shares

There's probably more confusion about shares than anything else in finance. To begin with, shares are also called stocks, capital stocks, equity capital, equities, and a few other things besides shares. Too bad, because the confusion is unnecessary. Shares are what the name suggests, a share of the company. Imagine you run a company and you want to expand to take advantage of the growing market. You could try to borrow the money, which you have to repay. If you offer people a share of the company, you don't have to pay it back. Instead, investors participate in the income stream of your company—the value of their share increases as the company and its income grow. For example, you might offer 10,000 shares at $10 each—it would raise $100,000 dollars and each share would represent one ten thousandth of the business. As the business makes profits, you can choose to pay dividends so the investors get an income. And if the business continues to do well, the shares are increasingly attractive (they are paying a nice income, and if the company is sound, they don't carry a lot of risk) so the price on each share tends to go up. And now, 10 years later, the share that was worth $10 initially is worth $1,000, so shareholders want to cash out; they will have a nice return.

There are refinements, like different classes of share, but we don't need to worry about those here; the essentials really are that simple.

In terms of our variables, shares tend to have a higher potential rate of return; you're effectively buying a share of an increasing future income (plus some potential gain in price). They're usually liquid, because there is a market for them. The amount is variable; there are shares that are relatively low priced and others that have quite a high minimum investment. It's when we get to risk that there's probably the most confusion. Put simply, this is an area full not of risk, but uncertainty. A sound bank or Government is unlikely to fold up, so cash or bonds are pretty reliable whatever happens. But the future income stream of a company is unpredictable, even companies that everybody is certain are winners can collapse (try looking up LTCM) and ones that they think are consigned to history can suddenly become world beaters again (look at the history of Apple).

The thing to remember is that, as with many features of investment, risk, return, and time are linked. People may tell you that shares are "risky" because they are not as certain as cash or bonds. But if you look at the long term (say, 10 years or more), there is one thing that you can be pretty much certain of, that in real terms, allowing for inflation, you won't make much, if any, profit from cash or bonds. By contrast, a company might do very well in real terms, or very badly, and with shares, you've got a piece of that so you might make a really attractive return, or lose your money entirely.

The useful point for our purposes is that, over a long term (five years at least, preferably a lot more), shares in strong companies are likely to give a *real return* better than cash or bonds, and although the *risk* is greater, it's not unreasonably greater *if* the *term* is long enough and the company really is sound.

## Property

There are several options with property. You can trade (buy and sell), develop (buy, convert, repair, and so on and sell), and also buy to let (or, in the United States, rent). Trading and developing are more like occupations—they take some time so if you're looking to grow funds while you do something else (like study!), you're probably going to be looking at letting. I mentioned this earlier in connection with the possibility of parents (or other relatives) buying a property to rent to you and your roommates, as a way to generate some income while also getting you a place to live.

The potential *rate of return* is high, which tends to mean that the minimum *amount* is also high—if the property offers a lot of income and capital growth, you will be competing with other people for it, and the larger the potential income, the larger the investment needed to buy. In the same way, the *term* tends to be long, even buying and selling can take months and renting for an income is generally a strategy that will run over years. For the same reason, property is *illiquid*; you can't simply turn it into cash in a hurry. And, as a consequence of those features, the *risk* can be high (even in the longer term; certainly in the short term). The returns can be fantastic, but you can also lose a lot of money; it's very hard to predict exactly what is going to happen and which way prices will go or how quickly.

So, those are the basics on investments. You can find much more detail in books about investing, and I'll add a few refinements as we go along, but we've now got an agreed language and some basic information to work with and for you to develop a money story and a savings and investments strategy that works for you.

From the definitions, you can see how the sort of investments you hold and the proportions of each can make a big difference to how well you achieve your goals. The proportions you hold them in is normally known as "asset allocation."

However, I'd suggest that you think of "asset allocation" in broader terms than just "so much in stock, so much in bonds, and so on." If you have a house, it's an asset. So is a car. Asset allocation is about the mix of all assets, where you hold them, how you hold them. And rather than thinking "what mix of shares and bonds should I have, how much in cash?," think "what do I want to achieve and when?"

## WHAT YOU WANT, NOT WHAT "MOST PEOPLE DO"

If you consider what you want, and work out when you want it and the required rate of return to get it by then, you can start to put together a plan. In general, that's likely to be based more on shares and/or property type investment for the long run and more bonds and cash and so on in the shorter term.

What's commonly done (what "most people do" or the general trend of financial advice) is to have allocations to the classes of assets based on your age or so-called life stage. Since you're young, that automatically means that the advice you'll get from most people is to invest most of your money in shares. Those same people would suggest that older people (your parents or grandparents, for example) should avoid shares (they're too risky short term) and to have nearly all their money in cash or bonds.

But that ignores what you want to do. I know some of you reading this book will start your own business and want to invest your money in that —you don't want a piece of somebody else's business; you want the whole of your own. And that others are going to have 1 career until you are 30 and then want to change direction, so you don't want to commit to the long term yet. You have a time horizon of perhaps 3–7 years, which is probably on the short side for big investment in shares. Similarly, there will be older people (they're allowed to read the book too!) who aren't planning on retiring to live on their investments in the next 5–10 years. I know plenty of professional people who are in their 50s or 60s who love what they do—Warren Buffett is in his 80s, and he's said he sometimes feels he should pay to be allowed to work; he loves his job so much. Those people are not going to retire any time soon unless they become too ill to work, so their time horizon for investment may be 20 years or more.

Too often, people follow advice to invest the way most people do, rather than investing to suit their circumstances and time horizon, so older people have mostly cash and bonds (which means that after inflation is taken into account, they'll end up with less than they've got now and can't afford the retirement they dreamed of), and the young people have money in shares that happen not to be worth as much just when they want the money for their new venture! Remember the doctor friend I mentioned earlier. He allowed the potential return (the money), to dictate what he did, so he invested in a way that was supposed to (and might actually) maximize his money in the long term. That made him worry about whether it was working in the short term. If he'd started by thinking about what he wanted and when, he might have worked out that he didn't have to do what the money wanted that made him nervous. He could use his money to get where he wanted, be in control, and be happy with what he was doing.

So when you're looking at decisions about how to allocate your money:

- Think about what all your assets are, not just the money you're investing now.
- Look at your own time horizon for your future plans.

Then you can make decisions about where to put your money and when you want to get at it that work for you.

## ADVICE, DIY, OR SOMETHING IN-BETWEEN

For savings, it usually makes sense to look at cash deposits for yourself. Again, ask yourself what is important to you: Do you prefer online banking or do you like seeing a human once in a while? Do you always go to the same branch or do you move all over, so a good ATM network is preferable? Do you use a debit card a lot? If you are receiving transfers of money (or your parents/grandparents are making deposits into your account), is it easily accessible to them? Find a bank that works for you! You can find out what accounts might be suitable by asking banks and looking online, and similarly check out how convenient they are for you where you'll be at college (is there a local branch if you need one) and compare interest rates.

If you want to get somebody to help, or you are handling longer term investments (bonds, shares, property) and want some advice, you're going to have to pay for that help and advice.

You can handle investment yourself, but if you're going to do that you do need to know what you're doing. I'll give some ideas for a DIY approach as we go, but if you're serious about totally doing your own investment, it's important to understand what the pros and cons are in a lot more depth than I'm able to describe here.

There are some other points I want to describe briefly now, because they'll make the descriptions of your choices easier in future. Those are *diversification*, *risk/reward ratio*, and *mutual funds*.

*Diversification* can sound quite complicated, but it's basically simple—it's the old adage of not having all your eggs in one basket. The classic idea is to make sure that if something happens that makes one thing you've invested in lose value, the same event will cause something else to go up—so on balance you don't have a calamity whatever happens.

Here's an example. Remember with bonds, they give a promise to pay back (redeem) the loan that the bond covers at some point (redemption date) and you get interest paid up to that point, plus the original loan value (par value). Remember also that the bonds are tradable; that's why they're liquid. If the coupon rate on the bond is higher than the rate you can get from a bank, the bond looks good—so it trades for a higher price. Take a bond that was originally $1,000 (par is $1,000), that will be paid back in 10 years, and that pays you 5 percent. Imagine after 5 years, interest rates generally are lower and a standard bank deposit account will only pay 2.5 percent. If you sell the bond, you'll probably get more than the "par" value because it's paying better than the market rate. Similarly, if interest rates available make the coupon rate on the bond look poor, the bond will trade at below the par value. The point is that the value that you sell a bond for can go up or down with interest rates, but the value goes in the opposite direction to general interest rates. So if interest rates go up, you earn more from cash deposits, but bonds tend to go down in value; if interest rates go down, you earn less from cash, and bonds tend to go up in value. Whatever happens, you've got something that gives you a gain.

There are masses of ways this works, but the key point is that this is what diversification is about; it's giving you a protection against everything you've got tanking at the same time.

*Risk/reward ratio* is about the linkage between risk and reward. It sounds logical and generally the idea that "no risk means no reward and high risk means exactly what it sounds like" holds. But do remember the point earlier; real life has uncertainty, not risk—it's very hard to know what the risk actually is, which the world found out in 2008 when most of the major economies suffered because investments that bankers and other "experts" thought were safe turned out not to be. There was a big reward for what they thought was a moderate risk, but actually the risk was huge and they didn't realize it.

*Mutual funds* are a way to get some diversification, with smaller amounts of money. Essentially, if you invest in one company (say you buy shares in Netflix), you do have a potential problem that if they do badly, they won't be able to pay a dividend, the shares will be less attractive and will drop in price, and you'll lose money. Even a really good company can have problems at least in the short term (life is uncertain, remember). The obvious way to deal with this is to buy shares in more than one company, but there's a limit to how much you can buy—especially when you are starting out. So funds are set up that buy a range of shares (in an industry, a sector, an area, and so on), and you can invest in the fund. You effectively get a little slice of each company the fund invests in.

So with investing, you can do it yourself directly, buy shares, bonds, property, and so on, either with or without taking advice from people.

You can also buy funds, which could be invested in shares in various industries, locations, and so on, could be involved in property, buy bonds, and so on, and as with buying directly, you do it entirely yourself, or you can get advice.

And you can hand over management to a greater or lesser degree, letting your advisor make some or all of the decisions.

Whichever way you go, there are a range of things to investigate and questions to ask; remember, this is your money!

## QUESTIONS TO ASK

When most people think of investment and management of money, they tend to focus on past performance and what the "market" thinks—remember our discussion of "rate of return?" I'm going to suggest some ways to find out more useful information and why they are useful. Whether you're doing it all yourself, getting advice, hiring managers, buying funds, or having somebody buy funds for you, I'd suggest that you look at matters in this order:

1. Charges and costs
2. Risk of loss (looking at potential and past losses and comparing them to what you are comfortable with)
3. The management style and qualities that the managers have
4. The ratings and past performance

Charges are a big issue. You know the power of compound interest and that one of the features of that is the interest rate. If you are paying, say, one percent charge a year for the advisor, one percent to the fund manager, and there are charges in the fund itself (to cover administration costs, taxes, transaction costs, and so on) of another one percent, you are losing three percent a year. If the investments you've made earn, say, five percent and inflation is two percent—well, I think you get the picture! It's worth remembering that fees and charges are usually payable irrespective of results—whether the advice you get is helpful or not and whether the investment you get is successful or not, you still pay for it.

So if you're doing it yourself, it makes sense to find a brokerage that charges minimal fees. If you're buying into funds, find ones that have the lowest charges.

That leads to another idea. If you are investing in funds, there is an option to buy "tracker" funds, ones that duplicate an "index." Indexes, like the Dow Jones or NASDAQ, are basically averages of the shares of lots of companies. Being averages, roughly half the shares in a particular area (the whole of the stock market, a sector, a geographical area, and so on) will do better than the index, and half will do worse. If you do the math on that, to beat the index 10 years in a row is a 1 in 1,024 chance (1 in 2, to the power 10), so it sounds unlikely. Therefore, a fund that beats its index for 10 years running would commonly be thought to be fantastically good. Since there are thousands of funds at a one in a thousand chance of doing it, you'd think a few ought to have a ten-year "beat the index" record every time. However, none do—there's a famous paper "Worse Than Chance" analyzing it and since then nobody has managed to show that the funds trying to beat the index can do as well as you'd expect them to do by luck alone.

A tracker fund buys the shares that make up the index, so it does "track" the index rather than trying to beat it. A lot of active managers don't like tracker funds—but compare their 10-year performance (net of fees) to a tracker fund and then decide. There's no evidence that anybody charging big fees to outperform trackers can actually do it.

The general level of fees on mutual funds, or management of funds, seems to be two percent (depending on asset class managed). The charges on tracker funds tend to be around 0.5 percent. So if you're not going to do all the research to pick shares yourself and you're either going to invest in mutual funds yourself, or get an advisor who will pick them or advise you how to pick them, I'd suggest you'd want a good reason to go into anything other than tracker funds. As Warren Buffett said, "Most investors, both institutional and individual, will find that the best way to own common stocks is through an index fund that charges minimal fees. Those following this path are sure to beat the net results (after fees and expenses) delivered by the great majority of investment professionals."[1]

One other point on costs. Sadly, you will probably be liable to tax on your gains, whether you take them as income or as a capital gain. So it makes sense to look at returns *net* of tax, rather than gross. That's the reason I said earlier that "a dollar saved is a dollar earned" is wrong.

A dollar saved is worth a full dollar; a dollar earned is likely to be reduced by tax—so the saved dollar is almost certainly worth more!

With risk of loss, I'd focus on loss, at least initially, rather than an abstract concept of "risk." That's because it isn't risk, it's uncertainty, so it's unquantifiable. Therefore the idea that a lot of advisors and fund managers have of "risk matched portfolios," matching what you invest in to your "risk appetite" or "risk profile," is largely a marketing exercise. They want you to buy on the basis of some pseudoscience that sounds great but is actually nonsense. You're usually better off getting an idea of the absolute worst-case scenario. It might be unlikely, but nobody knows how unlikely, so find out what the worst case is. If it happened, could you cope with it if you put all your investment in that area? If you couldn't, could you with, say, half the money? If so, then investing half the money in that investment and the other half in something that is not going to expose you to those losses (but that probably won't give you the same gains) may be sensible. It depends on what your required rate of return is!

Basically, this is another reason it's so important to know why you're investing and what your timescale is. If you know it's for the long term, for something important, it's easier not to panic. If you know you're looking long term, news like the share or property market you're investing in dropping drastically doesn't worry you. In fact if you're investing regularly, you get the benefit of "dollar cost averaging." You start to put in monthly amounts, the market drops, you buy at a lower price for a few months or years. In, say, 10 years' time, when the prices have gone up again, you've bought steadily and have more shares or property value than you would have done if you'd bought in a constantly rising market. So if you are clear on your values and goals, it's easier to ride the uncertainty without getting anxious and maybe making hasty decisions.

On the other hand, if you aren't sure what you want the money for, you'll be scared and you'll try to work out when to invest. You will try to time it for when prices are low, and you're quite likely to buy at the top of the market, when things are most expensive. If you need the money short term, in say, two years, you may well end up selling for less than you paid, because the share or property market has fallen just when you need the money. That's what could have happened to my doctor friend.

It's worth remembering with shares that you're buying a piece of a business. The idea is that you invest in it long term and get the reward for that as it grows long term. It's really about the fundamental value of the shares (Buffett is known as a "value investor"). However, the market overall mainly goes up and down not on value, but because people are trying to predict the short-term future. Imagine the stock market as being like a huge *America's got talent* show, where there's a prize for picking the winner. People don't necessarily vote for the best act; they vote for the one they think is going to win. Shares can get popular and go up way beyond what the business is actually worth (think of the "dot com" companies of a while ago). Others can go out of favor and go down. A lot of people (professional and amateur) try to guess what's going on (they don't call it guessing, but it is) and effectively gamble on their guesses about which way the market is going.

In assessing value, one thing Warren Buffett and just about every other successful investor looks at is the management structure: managers who control costs, who know their business, and who think long term. So it makes sense to look at the management of a business you're investing in directly, or fund management if you're going through funds, and pick ones that have a management style and philosophy that you understand and agree with.

The last thing to consider is fund past performance. There's a good reason for that, which I'll describe as we go on to some questions to ask potential advisors or fund managers.

You may be able to find potential advisors by asking friends and family. You can also look them up (and check them out) online to get a sense of what each firm is like. You can search for planners on the sites of the Financial Planning Association and the National Association of Personal Financial Advisors. The advisors on the latter organization's site are fee-only, meaning they will not earn commissions for selling you specific investments. Trouble is the fee often depends on how much you put with them. I've never understood myself why somebody is paid, say, $20,000 to manage $1 million, and $2,000 to manage $100,000. Having done that sort of thing, I never found there was more administration, research, advice, and so on; it was using bigger figures but it didn't take more time. And it was easier; with multimillionaires, I could buy whatever I wanted and get great diversification. When the amounts were smaller, I had to be more careful—they still expected the same gains but I didn't have the same scope to take risks with one investment as I didn't have the money to be able to balance it by diversifying elsewhere.

What you want is to know what you're paying and that your manager has your interests at heart. If managers can make commissions if you want something bought that pays them, and they can offset that against their fees (so you pay them less), that's great—but the big point is that you don't want surprises on costs and you want them to be working to make you money, not only to make themselves money.

Therefore, here are some questions that you might want to ask advisors, planners, fund managers, and so on before engaging them.

### 1. How do you charge for your services, and how much?

Apart from knowing, it helps you determine whether they have an incentive to sell you things. And you can look at how much the costs each year eat into any gains (called the "reduction in yield"), remember the compound effects!

### 2. Are you a fiduciary?

This question gets to having your interests at heart. A fiduciary will make decisions about what to buy and sell in your portfolio based on what is in your best interest. A nonfiduciary may be representing products that he is compensated for putting in your portfolio—even if they do not meet your goals.

### 3. What qualifications do you have?

You wouldn't use a doctor who wasn't qualified, why pay attention to a self-appointed "expert" from TV or the like, they've never had to take responsibility for any advice, and they've never had any independent assessment of their competence. For advisors, the Certified Financial Planner (CFP) qualification is harder to achieve than Chartered Financial Consultant (ChFC). If you want someone to manage your money, then look for a Registered Investment Advisor (RIA).

### 4. What services do you provide?

Go with someone whose offerings suit your needs. See whether they ask you questions and try to find out what you want. You want somebody who cares about your welfare, rather than seeing you as a source of income. And check what level of contact you get, a letter once a year, a meeting once a week, or whatever and make sure you can have what suits you. Also, whether you have a single regular contact or deal with a team and, again, go for what you feel comfortable with.

### 5. With what you'd suggest for investment, what is the worst-case scenario?

You can't get certainty about risk, but you can see if advisors appear to be honest about the dangers, and understand what you're trying to do, or whether they try to avoid the question and get you to take chances that definitely benefit them but might hurt you.

6. What's your investment approach and why?

If you want suggestions or management, and they are advising actively managed funds (ones that try to "beat the index"), ask them why. What performance advantage do they have, consistently, to offset the higher charges? If they give you examples of past performance, point out that this isn't a guide to the future; in fact, the funds that have been in the top range of performers in the past are, historically, more likely to be below average in the near future. And remember, everybody in finance can show their fund is wonderful, but only over a particular period or a particular fund out of the many funds that they have. Ask them what happened to all the other funds and for different periods and why they still have the funds that are clearly performing badly, why don't they just have the one that is doing well? And if one fund is so good, why is it only good over seven years and three months, what happens if you look at it over eight years or over six years six months? Are they just trading on a big jump because they got lucky at some point (which is what most of them are doing)? The point is that generally, they make more money on managed funds (whether they are ones they run themselves or ones they recommend), so you want to know whether there is a real advantage for you.

Remember, you ideally want things going up to balance what goes down. Some advisors do actually work on this, others will give you pseudoscience explanations involving efficiency frontiers, portfolio theory and complex sounding math. If they can't explain simply why it works, it probably doesn't work. Warren Buffett has joked that he ought to sponsor a chair at college to teach those theories, because it would mean that other advisors would get things wrong and make Mr. Buffett's investing job easier by handicapping his opposition![2]

If you want to handle investment yourself, you can—it really isn't terribly complicated, but it does take a lot of application to learn the basics, hard work to apply them, and organization to keep everything under control, so I'd only advise you to put in the effort if you really enjoy it and are prepared to dedicate a lot of time to it to start with, and monitor it regularly.

If you're going to get somebody else to help you, or to manage the investments, pick funds, and so on, start by being really clear on your values and goals, what you want, when you want it, your required rate of return, and so on. Then ask tough questions about the advice you get and why they suggest it (remember, again, this is your money!). If possible, take the advice to another "expert" for a second opinion—just like medical advice. You don't have to know much about it but just know what you want very clearly and know (as you do now) some of the ways that people may try to part you from your money. Then you can determine whether you would be paying for them to gamble with your money, or for giving you sound advice to achieve your values and goals and being paid a reasonable rate for professional expertise and for being honest.

## SUMMARY

Your money is your tool—start by thinking about yourself, what you need, what you want, and when you want it. Then think about how your money can help you and be a useful tool for you.

If you are saving for something (putting money aside), it's probably not the same as investing (getting it to grow for the future), but the labels are less important than what you are trying to achieve.

Five aspects that you should consider about investments are rate of return, risk, time, liquidity, and amount.

Think about "risk" versus "uncertainty."

Finding an advisor: An advisor should support you and your goals. Take time to find the right one if that is what you decide to do, and ask questions when you don't understand—until you do. Be a collaborator in building for your goals. And if you feel like you can do a better job, then go ahead and do it yourself—there are tools that make this possible. It will take time, and there is a learning curve you will need to come up, though.

## NOTES

1. Warren Buffett, Chairman's letter to the Shareholders of Berkshire Hathaway Inc., 1996, http://www.berkshirehathaway.com/letters/1996.html, accessed September 4, 2014.

2. Lawrence A. Cunningham, ed., *The Essays of Warren Buffett: Lessons for Investors and Managers Third Edition* (Singapore: John Wiley & Sons (Asia) Pte Ltd), 1995.

Chapter 9

# Setting Budgets and Making Financial Plans

I've thrown a lot of information at you in the last five chapters. I've tried to focus it to show that you are the important element and that all that other information is just to let you ask the right questions to get what *you* want. But much of it may be new and we talked about what happens to your brain when you're learning new things. Just know that if you are shell-shocked, you are in good company!

So, let's shift gears and tap in to your creativity. Get a pen and paper (tablet, laptop, and so on) and set aside 20 minutes. Now ask yourself: What would you do if you won a lottery prize of $50 million—what would make you happy?

No self-editing—just let your mind go, no matter how "crazy" it sounds ("crazy" is the chance that you might actually win the prize!). Write down the first 15 things that come to mind. Be as specific as you can (e.g., if you want a house, what sort, how big, what would it have in the way of facilities, where—exactly—would it be?). If you'd invest the money, how much? All of it? Who would manage it? How much income would you want? What would you do with that income? Would you have a yacht, a private jet, holiday homes around the world, a fleet of cars? Most of all, have fun with this.

After 20 minutes, look at the list and see where the desire for each item on it has come from: "someone else has one," "this is what I should want," "I always said 'when I grow up I want. . . .' " Now separate the list into three "buckets": things you feel you *should* want if you have

$50M, things someone else (family, friends, and so on) thinks you would want if you have $50M, and things (or activities) that you really want in your life. For example, do you feel that if you're a millionaire you have to have a big house—like the one you've seen in *Hello* or *Town & Country* magazine? Do you want a Ferrari because the guy in high school you always competed with bragged about the Firebird his father got him?

Now, count up the things that come from the media "image" ideas that you hear and see in advertisements. Compare that to the things driven by competition with friends and family (to prove you're the best) or enemies (to shut them up), the stuff that "experts" or advisors have told you that you ought to want, the ones you've been sold, the ones that your parents want. Finally, add up the ones that could fulfill your dreams, ones that you would truly value and be happy about long term. What do you notice?

With clients I tend to make a little graph of it—because a picture really is worth 1,000 words—with labels like "it's expected of millionaires," "experts say," "compete with friends and family," "shut up idiots," "parents expect," and so on. It depends on what drove you to put it down in the first place. The only common label is "I really would love."

And that "I really would love" column is nearly always the shortest!

Most people only have one or two things that they really want, that will make them happy. And isn't that telling! Given the choice to imagine what creates happiness, without any money constraints, people usually choose to buy mostly things that other people think they should have or that they've been told they should want, often because they are not really clear on what they want for themselves.

I don't want that for you. I want you to make decisions about your money that make yours a really happy life, and one that is successful *in your terms*. So now, stand up, take a breath and walk around the room, then come back, and write a list of 7–15 things that you would do/have/give if you won $50M.

Remember in Chapter 1 we talked about a life you could be proud of, what you'd tell your favorite interviewer. Wouldn't it be great if you could have that life?

That's what this chapter is about: using your money as a tool to build the life you want and are proud of. Wherever you are starting, with a little or a lot, you can build toward the life you want and have fun doing it.

So I'm going to talk about putting together everything we've talked about and building a financial plan that will get you where you want to go—to use your money to create your ideal life and not spend your life chasing after money for money's sake or to surround yourself with things that don't matter to your dreams. I'm going to use one example to illustrate how one client and I worked to put together a plan. You may find that your details are different, but I know you're smart so you can take the principles in the example and apply them to yourself. You don't need me to spoon-feed you.

Remember Terri, who wants to be an architect? Let's look at how she put her financial plan and some budgeting together.

Terri is clear what she wants to do, the courses she's interested in, and what things will cost (check back to Chapter 1 if you need to refresh). And they all involve her moving away from home.

Like Angela (in Chapter 2), Terri's money story is based on money being a tool and being discussed openly in her family. Her father worked his way to owning a small store and knew that in business, and life, he had to keep costs under control and plan ahead. Neither of Terri's parents had the opportunity to go to college, but they appreciated the advantages. They were both very happy in what they did and above all wanted Terri, her brother, and sister to be happy.

From early on, the children understood the relationship between responsibility and money. All of the children had small jobs (they'd help out in the store, do paper rounds, act as sitters for neighbors' kids when they were old enough). They were involved in planning expenditure and family holidays, which gave Terri a grasp of the reality of income and expense (the mechanics of money). What she didn't have were particular practical skills. She was the most academic of the siblings, read a lot, and liked organizing projects. Her sister Kate, on the other hand, was fascinated when their mother would alter dresses or suits, run up overalls for her husband from scrap material, and even make curtains and loose covers for the house (and for friends). Terri saw the value of this: Money she spent on clothes would be money she wouldn't have for her course, or for other things she wanted. She also realized that if she learned some skills then, like her mother and sister, she could either trade for other things she wanted, by helping other people to adapt clothes, or perhaps she could earn extra money doing small repairs and tailoring. So she pestered her mother and sister, who were actually delighted to be in demand, for instruction and practice in doing some of the basics, in the year before she was due to go to college.

Terri wasn't expecting to be as good at dressmaking, alteration, and so on as her sister (let alone her mother, who had been doing it for longer and had far more experience). But she knew that if she applied herself she would be good enough to have a useful skill to trade. She considered other things that would be useful, like cooking (her father and brother had got interested in nutrition, so they both loved to cook healthy, balanced meals), but decided that her "architect's eye" could see things like style and design in sewing. And the challenge of turning something drab into something beautiful would give her the motivation to stick with learning when sometimes it got hard or tedious.

She also deliberately *unlearned* some things. Terri realized that a part of her money story was that it was always wrong to spend money on herself—money had to be for "useful" things. Gifts for family or family holidays were OK, but things purely for Terri were not. Her parents never actually said as much, and her brother and sister didn't get that bit of the money story, but that's what Terri had heard and what she had told herself for years. She knew when she was away she'd have to learn to cut herself some slack, to be a little bit self-indulgent sometimes—but the way her money story ran, that would trip her up every time. So she deliberately worked on rewriting that story by designing a little experiment. She asked adults she knew what they did purely for themselves. She started with her parents, asking what they did for themselves, and found that they each, in different ways, allowed for some indulgences; some little elements of time or money that allowed them to live a happy life without feeling imprisoned or deprived. Then she talked to other adults she knew and she found that all of them had little indulgences, ways to spend time and money on themselves. Some felt they overdid it, some kept it on plan, but nobody totally ignored themselves. So Terri persuaded herself—allowed herself—to change that aspect of her money story. She was able to rewrite her story so by the time she was getting her first-year plan for college into its final shape, she was able to build in some "me time" and some "fun money" as a necessary expense. Terri knew what her values were, so she knew she wouldn't be completely self-indulgent, but realized, in checking her money story, that the message about not spending on herself had come from her own interpretation, rather than a fact that her parents or family had relayed to her.

You can do the same; know what you really need to live a happy life and be aware of your money story and, as Terri did, experiment with ways to change it where necessary if you realize your story doesn't fit the facts. The point is to know what your story is now, so you can be clear on your own values and use them as a filter to change your behavior so that it works for you, not against you.

We talked in Chapter 3 about Terri's goal to get work during vacation. She succeeded in that and moved on to the next step to get her where she wanted to be, to start planning her first year, and particularly the first semester (this is important: break things into manageable time frames).

The initial thing was to budget for the "needs" of living at college, which meant fees, housing, and food.

Terri first had to decide which college was most interesting to her: She had three options. One of the "popular science" books Terri had read that got her interested in studying architecture had been written by a professor at one of the colleges. Terri thought it would be great to study with her, maybe go on to do postgraduate study with somebody that she already thought of as a role model. So Terri checked it out. She did an online tour, visited the campus, asked questions, made some contacts. And she checked what classes the professor taught, how easy it was to get onto those, the access to the professor if she were on the course, the book lists that were required, and basically got all the information she could. She also visited the other two colleges (she wasn't going to let the "wow factor" persuade her to make rash decisions) and she thought she could be happy at any of them. They all had pros and cons, but she decided that the one where *her* professor lectured was the one she'd like best. It had some factors she wasn't so keen on—the dorms she'd be in were a bit of a way from the lecture theater she'd use the most, and they didn't have so much emphasis on the sports she liked (she was a keen swimmer and the pool facilities were a bit meager), but it did have a really active social setup, a great library, and it was near enough to an interesting city that had buildings that she learned were used in some of the architecture courses.

Terri was quite keen to have her own place and be independent, but her favorite college insisted that first-year students live in dorms. So she checked out the costs and also arranged on a visit to stay over with a *buddy* to see what they were like and how it worked in practice. The policy was that the first-year rooms had similar facilities (which included the things that Terri really cared about), they were single gender (which she was happy about—for now), but she did have a choice of two- or four-person dorms and completed a questionnaire about herself that was used to match her with roommates. The four-person rooms were cheaper (she has to share facilities with more people), and as she was used to competing for a bathroom with parents and siblings, that was no problem. She also liked the prospect that with four, there would be more contacts, more ideas.

She had been involved in the family budgeting for years and knew what it involved. An advantage of the setup in the dorm was that a lot of the basic things were taken care of; Terri knew that utilities, maintenance, and so on were an extra distraction and pressure, and while she settled in, it was probably better to be able to concentrate on finding her feet in the college, learning where things were and making contacts, and studying, of course!

So the rent was the first basic that came off the total amount available. It covered much of the list of housing expenses in Chapter 4, including utilities, furniture, maintenance, cleaning tools (and most of the consumables). She'd still need to make sure there were some supplies of consumables and all her own personal stuff (toothpaste, hair products, and so on), but there was a lot less shopping to arrange with her new roommates.

She was starting to get her basic expenses organized, the next thing being to arrange a food plan. But first she wanted to make sure she had a way to handle the regular expenses and make sure any bills to be paid were paid on time. She was well organized, so she was used to having "to do" lists and marking things in her diary on her phone. (If you are usually not well organized, find something that works for you to keep track of things like paying bills—it will make life much simpler.) Terri spoke to her dad about accounts and setting up standing orders for regular bills. Having run the store, he was very familiar with everything related to banks (charges, services, telephone banking, and so on). But he was used to having a set of paper accounts, backed up on the computer. Terri was more used to working on computer, tablet, or phone and sometimes having paper back up. So she got some recommendations from her dad and family friends, spoke to the college about the accessibility of different banks, and made a shortlist. Then she checked with the banks and compared services (ATM, charges, overdraft coverage, free checking, online services, and so on). She wasn't planning on using credit—not yet anyhow—but thought it could be useful for emergencies. She needed to get her parents to cosign on the credit card, which wasn't a problem, and she deliberately had a low credit limit so she could cover emergencies, but not be tempted to splurge!

The various charges for services all went into the budget. Terri chose to make a simple spreadsheet with her income as one line and all the expected expenses as deductions. (There are a lot of budgeting apps you can choose from; they tend to be a lot of work to set up with your expense items, so a spreadsheet is usually simplest!)

And because she wanted to do her banking electronically, she needed good phone and Internet links that were very secure. So she spoke both to the bank that provided what she wanted and to the college IT department and made sure of her security—and added charges for antivirus, backup (to cloud), security, and any banking and other apps she needed to the budget.

With most of the necessary expenses around housing now covered, Terri had to build in the costs around tuition. These were largely fixed; there wasn't much she could do to reduce them. She checked on the health insurance that was required and she was covered adequately by her parents' policy until she would have left college. That was a saving, and she contacted the college and got a waiver for the policy that she would have been charged for.

She checked on book lists for the first year to see what they would cost her. She'd already suggested to her relatives that as birthday presents they might want to give her money for things she needed or, for those who wanted to buy her something, she made a wish list where she put some of the books she knew she'd want to keep. But in contacting the college, and her newly assigned roommates, she found that there was a collective buying scheme that some of the sophomores started a few years ago. For some courses she could get access to copies of the main texts and share the costs among several of her new classmates. They would then be able to pass the books on to the next year's freshmen (assuming they hadn't gone out of date). Terri thought that was a great idea and looked at what was available for her courses, also attempting to contact some of the people who would be on the course to see if they would be interested in sharing the costs of some of the books. So now she had a rough idea of her book costs for her budget. Other than books, there wasn't a lot that she'd need that wasn't provided as part of the tuition, or that she didn't already have access to.

She discovered that there was the possibility of being able to do a study course in Europe in the final year. It was a scholarship program and places were limited, but if she could get on it, she could get the scholarship funding (if her grades were good enough). She calculated that even with funding, she would need to put in some funding herself.

Useful goal #1: See whether it was at all possible to get the scholarship and save or raise the additional funds and, if so, to plan how to do it.

Before that, she needed to sort out all the other expenses so that she knew exactly what money she had to spare.

Housing and fees taken care of, the next need was food. It seemed sensible to go for most of her meals in the college dining service. She contacted her new roommates and, while checking out some basics of what they liked, what rules they were going to adopt, and so on, found that one was actually quite keen on cooking. However, what was allowed in the rooms was pretty limited, and since neither Terri nor any of the others actually knew whether the girl was just keen, or actually a good cook, it was both more economical and safer to opt for the meal plan! They all, including the keen cook, thought that was a sensible start; after a semester, they could opt for more "home cooking" or other options if they got bored with the food or if they found a cheaper way to do it. But the food plan seemed quite good for making contacts and took some of the anxiety out of budgeting and finding decent meals. It didn't mean they'd got to eat together all the time, but it gave them some potential company if they wanted, and it was something they could all share in, at least at the start. Terri built in some money to her budget for snacks, coffees, and a meal or two a week that she could decide on at the time. She based it on what she knew of costs for what she liked to eat, and she checked places near to campus to get an idea on pricing.

She also agreed with her roommates on some basics of chores. They would sort out a proper rotation when they got there, but they initially agreed to keep the common areas tidy, which meant not leave drying clothes hanging in the bathroom or coats and shoes lying around in the living space; take turns with cleaning; and so on, and they agreed to leave one another's private space private and not borrow anything without asking or complain if somebody's own space wasn't kept the way they would keep their own. They also swapped some ideas of what they were like (since Terri liked to organize, she volunteered to do the cleaning schedule, and the keen cook volunteered to cook a welcome meal during their first week). They discovered that two of them were used to doing their own laundry, ironing, and so on and two weren't, so Terri immediately found some skills that she could pass on and be helpful to some of the others. Terri also discovered that her newfound sewing skills could be a good way to make some extra money, which was very handy, because the next decision Terri made was that it was going to be really difficult to afford to run a car if she wanted to be able to do other things, particularly to save for the course abroad. She sat down with her father and went through the checklist of expenses for the car (Chapter 6) and realized, objectively, that the cost was too high. In the short run, she could run a car and do what she wanted if she took out a big loan, but that would mean, in the longer run, the loan interest would be mounting up all the time, and she would limit her choices (e.g., to do postgraduate work).

Two of her new roommates were planning on having cars, so, assuming that she could build a good relationship with them (and having some useful skills to trade), she felt that there was no reason she'd be really restricted. It was a pain not having her own car, but it was a big expense, and there were so many other important things she needed that it simply didn't justify the opportunities she'd have to give up (or the debt she'd have to take on) to have a car.

That meant that she did need alternative transport. The things she'd need for the first semester were reasonably accessible, so she thought her bike would be fine to get around the campus. She checked and there was secure storage at all the main buildings for bikes, so she got a secure lock for the bike, got it serviced, and arranged for it to go with her when she went to college (it cost a bit to freight it there, but she wouldn't need to transport it back home every vacation).

That brought her to thinking about costs for traveling to and from college and home, and any money she'd need for public transport, shuttle service, and cabs. The travel home was reasonably predictable; she had arranged the vacation job, which, fortunately, was near enough home to stay at home during the whole period, so she knew what the fares were. Any public transport costs were more of an unknown. With the bike, and the possibility of being able to get lifts from her roommates with cars, Terri didn't think she'd have too many costs, but she didn't want to have a hole in the budget that she hadn't provided for. So she put a section of her budget into a different account—and this is a good time to look at how she did that, as an example of what you can do.

She had one account for the known, necessary expenses. This was for her rent, tuition, food, share of any household expenses she'd agreed, phone, computer, and so on, things that she knew she absolutely had to pay or there would be real problems. That money was not to be touched for anything else (in the next chapter, we'll talk about tactics for keeping the "needs" budget protected).

She also had a "working money" account. That's where the money for occasional meals, snacks, travel expenses, personal items (cosmetics, for example) went. That was tricky to judge in advance, because the amounts might vary from week to week (or even day by day): sometimes she wouldn't spend any money on some items for months; other times she would spend a lot in one go. So her estimate/guess at what she might spend, on average, on cabs, shuttle, and public transport went into her working money account.

Also in that budget went a lot of the personal care items, shampoo, toothpaste, skincare items, haircut service, and so on. Terri wasn't terribly fussy about most of those, but she was particular about her hair. So she was willing to allow for name brand products that worked for her—and economize on other items. She also liked to have her hair properly cut and had a stylist near home that she liked. She knew what that cost, but she figured she couldn't just leave her hair for times when she was home and could make an appointment, so she decided to check out salons around the campus and get recommendations. So some money went into the plan for three or four sessions with her favorite (for Terri, this was a "necessary" expense), and some money went into the working account as an allowance for another stylist to keep her going in term time.

Terri knew that if she was going to work effectively (particularly if she wanted to have a chance at that scholarship and the trip abroad), and if she wanted the energy to socialize effectively, she needed to eat well and to exercise. She'd built in some good nutrition and wanted to match it with some exercise. She'd be doing more cycling than she'd done, and there was not only a gym at the school but miles of pathways that she could run on. She did figure she'd miss her main sport, swimming, because the pool wasn't that great. She found the college was starting a triathlon club, which would be ideal, because they were going to use a local pool for training that gave better facilities. It did mean some expenses, and fitting into the appropriate training times, but it gave her a range of exercise, loads of new contacts, and therefore social experiences, transport to and from the pool, help with bicycle maintenance, and technique and coaching on all three disciplines (swim, bike, run!). Terri wasn't sure she was really interested in competing seriously, but as a low-cost way of keeping fit, a social outlet, and a potential hobby, it was hard to beat.

She also needed to allow for clothes and accessories. At the start, she'd got all the clothes she needed, but she wanted to build in flexibility as well as replacement items and "special occasion" clothes.

Terri was smart enough to know that it can take some experience and experiment to find out how to buy well but economically, and she didn't really have the money to be able to afford mistakes. So she asked one of her aunts, who was keen to give her an "off to college gift" to fund a trip to a major clothing store that provided personal shoppers. Terri wanted to gain experience of where it was worth paying for quality materials and cut (suits, dresses, sweaters, for example) and where she could econo-mize with cheaper things (some belts, tee shirts, for example). She ended up much more ready to ask for information, try things, experiment, and (because of her acquired dressmaking skills) be able to adapt.

It meant that some things that were fundamental and would need to be of real quality went into the "necessary" expenses—they'd be fairly rare, but they were predictable. More everyday items, replacements, bargains that would get used a lot went into the "working" account. And thanks to the shopping advice and some experiment, Terri could make a reason-able estimate of how much, on average, she would spend even though this would vary in the short term.

Finally, there was an allowance for the impractical but irresistible dress for the party!

This was tricky to estimate, so I asked Terri about some of the best social experience she'd had, what she did. A typical one was when a group of friends went out and did a bit of window-shopping around the fancy designer shops, rented a DVD, got some pizza, and ended up with an impromptu party. We worked out what her share of the cost was and that gave us a base figure for a good evening.

Your ideal social time might be totally different, but you can work out what it costs. Do include everything, entrance money, cab costs, food costs, and so on. That gives you a base figure.

With Terri, we worked out what that figure was and made that the allowance of "fun money" for a week. Not every week is going to be the same, but as long as it worked out that she didn't blow all the budget and had a limit, she was comfortable. So if she had a week when she'd watched some movies, gone to a party, bought a dress, and spent nearly three weeks allowance in a week, she knew that for the next two weeks she really had to avoid spending anything much from the "fun money" account. That wouldn't always be easy (sometimes it would be very hard), but Terri knew that it would work and that way she stayed on plan—she was using the money to have the life she wanted.

She wanted to include in the "necessary" expenses some charity dona-tions, but looking at the figures, it did look very tight on budgets. So Terri decided to give some time instead to local charities, looking into what sort of activities were available locally to the college and finding that the col-lege was actively involved in supporting various charities through both donations and practical help. She thought that was good; it was helping people without it eating into her budget. She did have a momentary worry that the feeling that you're saving money isn't a very worthy motivation for a selfless act. However, we decided that using some spare time to play video games (that she'd bought and thus wouldn't cost her anything) was an alternative use of time and if instead she helped other people for no financial reward, she was doing something worth more to the charity than the tiny financial contribution that she could have made.

The other things that she needed to include in the budget were events, such as Christmas, holidays, and birthdays. There wasn't a lot of expense she needed to allow there; her family weren't expecting her to give them presents and bring back items. She knew that (although they wouldn't admit it) her brother and sister were quite envious of her going away to college and she made sure to keep them up to date through Facebook and calls, and she brought back some college items for them. She also kept some of her A-grade papers to show her parents—she knew her father wouldn't say anything, just smile, but he'd be more pleased with that than if she'd bought him a new truck.

She did ask for things she needed as presents, as with her aunt and the shopping trip. One thing was that she took pictures of a suit that she saw that would be perfect for her vacation job; it was really classy and powerful, but elegant. There was no way that she could afford it, but she made some notes on the material, cut, and so on and passed them on to her mother and sister.

So, the bulk of the budget and the costs for housing, food, necessary and optional expenses were covered. She made sure of the essentials, built in some fun, minimized the need for debt, and used all the resources that Terri had. And now she could go back and review her savings goal #1: the potential study course in Europe in the final year.

This was something that she'd need to plan for in the same way as she had in getting the vacation job—it wasn't a simple "try and see."

First of all, she looked at the possibilities if she couldn't get the full scholarship. She realized she could do it—if she lived on bread and water for three years, never went out or spent any money, and worked two or three part-time jobs as well as the vacation job! But by then, she wouldn't be able to think straight enough even to pass, let alone get good grades, and she'd go insane, so that was no answer.

So she had to decide whether she was going to make sure she put in the work to give herself the best chance of getting the scholarship award. That's not trivial; it's got an opportunity cost, like everything else. There would be no point missing out on social events, turning down invitations, passing up the chance to do things because she really needed to study, and doing all that for a couple of years, then deciding it wasn't worthwhile—that would be to waste all that experience she'd passed up for nothing.

She decided it was worthwhile and told her family and her roommates that this was what she was going to do. Telling people about your goals is a powerful tool; we'll look at it in more detail in the next chapter, but it's basically part of the goal being "noted," which brings us to our mnemonic for goals. Hopefully, you've got your own version, but the one I use is CHEAP SMART PLAN and noted is the final N.

Let's look at the goal, in the way that Terri and I did.

She wanted to get this trip to Europe, which means that she needed the scholarship for the marks to qualify and also for the funding. She also needs to put in an amount herself.

In the long term, this is part of her value of being a great architect. It would be fantastic experience and terrific for her résumé. It would also be a real achievement and proof to herself as much as anybody else that she really "has what it takes." So it's certainly going to make her happy in the long term and be exciting for her in the short term. And those things are aligned; working toward the marks for the exams and saving up the money for the trip are all going the same way.

It is positively worded; she wants to win the scholarship and be able to go on the trip to Europe—there's no "I want to avoid" negatives in there; it's all "this is the situation I want to be in."

And she can put in the work and save the money so she's got control—although with investment (which she might need), she can't entirely control the return she gets. So that's the "cheap" part of the mnemonic.

There's also a very clear timescale, the trip is in the final year, so it's three years away. Terri can set some intermediate goals for both the study and the savings to make sure she's on track (it's measurable), and she can set those goals by semester, year, or whatever she likes.

With the scholarship, it's possible to find out what sort of marks she'll need. It's impossible to control the exact marks she'll get, but she can practice with past papers and make sure she works on assignments to get them at least to the standard—it's certainly pretty specific and she has ready-made measures of progress with term papers, assignment marks, and so on. The scholarship is also adaptable: If she's way over the marks, great, she doesn't ease off but it gives her a bit of cushion. And she's got the resources, she's obviously got the intelligence and most important she's got the motivation, she knows why she's doing this, it really matters to her, and if more effort is needed, she'll make that effort.

That's the whole of the "smart" part of the goal for studying, but with the money, there's a bit more involved.

The goal is specific; she can work out what money is needed in addition to the scholarship (if the costs go up, the scholarship will cover the increase). It's measurable, because she can work out how much she needs to put away each month, week, or whatever and see whether she's on target or not. It has to be worked out on the basis of savings, not of total value of course, because the growth of any saving or investment isn't controllable. That's the involved part, because knowing whether the resources are adequate may depend on how much needs to be put away and how much it may grow. But the plan is adaptable: If things work out well, then Terri might be able to put away less money or reach the target sooner than expected; if things go badly, she might have to put away more (she can't give herself more time; the time is fixed).

So what are needed are the elements of "plan," the little steps, the specific plans (not hopes), the actions that will get her there, and the recording and telling of what is going to happen.

For the scholarship part, it's relatively easy for Terri, because scheduling work is something she's done in high school. She works better with a timetable and knowing when she's supposed to do things. It's more difficult than high school because the work is unfamiliar, so she's not so sure how long tasks will take. Similarly, undergraduate work is more "vague"; there is more scope to do it your own way than in high school. Terri is used to having very clear definitions of what is wanted, what a *good* paper looks like; now she's got less framework and structure, and she has to make more decisions about exactly how to present things, should it be "compare and contrast" or "critique," and so on. But she built in time to discuss with professors and students with more experience and came up with a plan that allowed her to take little steps, build her knowledge and experience, and get feedback so that she can adapt if necessary. And these are all based on her actions; there's no waiting for other people to do things.

The money is harder for her. She knows what the target is and when the money is needed. But she can't simply put in more effort to get more money; she knows it's counterproductive to try to work 24/7 at study and part-time jobs and be able to keep that up. So she keeps to the budget she's got and works out how much can be put away, looks at the earnings she can get from the vacation job and from doing a bit of term time work, doing some trades with people to save some money, using gifts of money from relatives, and so on. And it still doesn't reach the amount she needs.

That's where there's an easy, and for Terri dangerous, option. She could simply push all her "fun money" into the savings budget. That would make it up to what she needs. But she knows her past money story; she knows she finds it easy to neglect herself and her fun—and being like that is not being what she wants to be or a healthy way to be. If she does that, she'll be obsessive, dedicated entirely to saving money, and forget about all the great experiences and all the fun of college.

So she looks at how she can save, maybe she doesn't need the hair stylist, maybe there are other economies she can make. But again, that's not being true to herself, she doesn't insist on much for herself, it's something that she really wants and went into the "necessary" costs, it's got to be nonnegotiable. She goes over the budget, moves things around a little, and there's still not quite enough.

So there are a couple of options. She can just give up and decide it's not possible to pay for the trip. She can try to invest the money to make up the shortfall from a bit of growth. Or she can potentially borrow some money.

Now when you come to decisions like this, you have to make your own choices. Your situation will be different, but the basics are the same, you have necessary expenses and optional expenses, and a small part of those optional ones are "fun" and basically necessary if you are going to remain sane. You have to decide on the balance, what's your Goldilocks point, what is too much self-indulgence, what is too much denial, and what is "just right?" And how do you deal with the other things that you are setting goals for, how do you balance all the demands on your money to get the right solution for you?

I can't tell you what you should do, but I'll tell you what Terri decided.

She really wanted that trip, and she was very close. So she looked at the figures and found she needed about three percent a year return on her money to be able to fund it. That included having a reasonable budget for living, a bit of fun and being sociable, time to do some charity work and to do plenty of studying, but also time to develop friendships and enjoy the experience of college.

She talked to her father and a couple of other trusted people about investing and found that if she invested the money she saved each month in cash deposits and bonds she'd make a bit of a profit, but it wouldn't quite be enough.

She got some financial advice and came up with this plan. She'd put an amount away each month, separate from her other accounts. This would get invested in a low-cost index-tracking fund. That meant most of the money was being invested. Three years was a very short term for that sort of investment, it might work out very well, but the market might fall sharply and she'd end up with less money than she started with just when she wanted it to fund the trip. But she had a plan for that. She was putting the money in regularly, so if the market fell she'd benefit from dollar cost averaging; she'd buy the units in the fund at a lower average price. Eventually (over perhaps 5 to 10 or more years) the market would pick up (this was part of her advice and research) and the overall return was hopefully going to be better than the 3 percent a year that she needed.

The plan had some flexibility; if the investment worked and gave her the three percent, great. If it made more, then she'd either be able to leave the money to grow further, or she'd have some extra spending money for the trip. If it had grown, but not enough, she could take out a loan for the difference—she didn't want a loan, but it should be a very small one by then; it was for a very good cause and by the time she needed the loan, she would be near graduating—so she expected she was going to be in a position to earn a wage and start paying the loan back. And if the market had really fallen, she could take out a loan (although that would be really worrying) on the basis that the market would recover at some point and that it should cover the loan plus interest, given the average growth of that type of fund over periods of 10 years or more.

It wasn't absolutely ideal; life doesn't always give us the ideal option, but it gave her a plan that she could control and that gave her a good chance of achieving what she wanted, without having to give up things that she really couldn't do without. And there was another possibility. If she made a good impression with the architect's firm she was working for in the vacation, she might be able to approach them about financing the balance of her trip.

That's how it worked for Terri. And what this example shows is that the common idea of "make a budget, you should be able to live on X" and "set your SMART" goals is more simplistic than real life. Budgets are a guide for you to get to your goals. If your budget feels like a straitjacket, step back and review what is so confining. Remember, it is a tool to getting you where you want to go. So make it a tool that works for you and, especially when you are starting out, review your assumptions to make sure they are still right: Are your transportation estimates too high and your fun estimates too low? Then adjust them to reflect your reality!

## SUMMARY

Know what you really want for yourself; try the "won the lottery" exercise to make sure it is for you.

Look at your necessary and optional expenses and prioritize the necessary ones.

Do your research; find out what you can economize on and what you can't.

Use your bank accounts: "necessary," "working," "fun," and so on.

If you need to plan for goals, use CHEAP SMART PLAN (or your own version of it) and work out how you'll get there.

Chapter 10

# Changing Habits and Behavior

This chapter is about *how* you can make changes to get the life you want.

You're aware of your money story and your own habits now. You know that you would be better off financially if, instead of going for retail therapy when you are upset, you took a walk or that if you could get organized to balance your checkbook each month, you'd be in charge of your money instead of feeling like it was in charge of you. And you know that if you could remember to pay bills on time to avoid fees and interest, you wouldn't leak so much money. And knowing where you are is the first step to changing.

So, let's talk about how you can manage to do things that at the moment seem like too much effort. You're clever, you know things like planning ahead, setting goals, not wasting money, and so on are what can get you where you want to go—but "life" seems to get in the way of your plans! We'll start with playing to your strengths: keeping with things you find easy, and developing ways that work for you to change things you find hard and make them "just what I do."

There are three things you need to know about changing your habits or behaviors.

1. Changing is always possible.
2. Changing is often difficult.
3. Changing may require different actions at different times, and what works for somebody else may not work for you and what works for you at one time may not work at another.

You may have tried to change things before, maybe lose weight, get your school work organized, or tidy your room—sometimes you make it; sometimes you don't. The reason you don't isn't about willpower, no matter what you hear. The reason is you didn't use tactics that work for you, at the right time, and persist with them for long enough. You'll probably have to do a bit of work to find out the best tactics for you in the current situation and then persist a bit, but you can definitely change. Knowing your values and using them as your foundation will be a huge help in sticking with what you need to do if it gets hard.

It would be great if there was a magic formula to change any habit or behavior that always worked, whoever you were, whatever your situation. That's why most best-selling lifestyle books become best sellers—we all want an easy "fix," a magic formula for success. There is no magic formula. But you can build a muscle of success by identifying what you need to do, when you need to do it, and sticking with it.

Let's start with ways to work out where you are now and what that means for changing. Then we'll look at the sort of things that you may need to do to change and how to turn that into specific behaviors that you need to perform to get the changes you want. And finally, I'll give you ways to assess your success as you go along and fine-tune as you need to.


## WHERE YOU ARE NOW

What I'm talking about here comes from the transtheoretical model of change. The theory came out of research into health, specifically with addiction. The research found that if you looked at where people started, it was easier to pick out things that would help them change successfully than if you tried to find a "one size fits all" solution, whatever the client situation. And this technique works for changing financial behavior. You can look it up; there are masses of studies and a couple of good popular books about it. We talked about this before: Until you know where you are, it will be difficult to get where you want to go!

I've simplified the full model, because you don't need it all, you just need to get an idea of what "stage of change" you're in. The stages are related to where you are with a problem: trying to recognize what's not working (*contemplation*), knowing something needs to change but not knowing how to sort it out (*preparation*), not having a coordinated set of actions that work together (*action*), and having made some changes not being sure of how to stick with them (*maintenance*). Let's see where you may be.

## Contemplation

Some common thoughts at this stage: "I'm thinking about changing my money story and habits but I'm not sure about what to do or what I need to change." "I don't seem to know where my money goes, but there is never enough of it for what I want to do." "I seem to have trouble paying for things like my phone bill but I'm never sure why." "I often spot things I want but don't have the money for them." "I want/have a credit card but I'm a bit concerned what I'll do with it." "I'm not sure what life I'd want if I did suddenly get money." "I'm not sure how I'd set out a budget or decide on my priorities if I had to." "I'd like to handle my money better but don't know what things to change."

## Preparation

And here: "I'm getting a bit worried about money and going to college; I don't have a plan." "I got a budget plan but I can't stick to it." "I can't make up my mind; I plan to save and then decide I want to spend the money instead!" "I've been looking into ways to cut back, and looked at some of the ideas so far in the book." "I've done a couple of things like try to set priorities for needs and optional, but I'm not sure whether it is really making much difference." "I need to talk to my parents—or somebody—about questions I have about money, but it never seems like the right time!" "I'm trying to get control but I keep going round in circles with the problem."

## Action

"I drew up my own budget; now how am I going to make it work!" "I feel as if I'm saving for the future and not living in the present!" "I've spoken to my parents about making more of a contribution to the household, what else do I do?" "I've started to get a grip on my phone and clothes bills and banned myself from shopping, maybe for a month." "I know I need to sort my finances out, so I'm trying to write everything down for a month so I can keep track." "I've started to focus on what I really want to achieve in life but I keep getting sucked back into chasing short-term things to compete with people at school." "I've set some goals and determined some priorities, but they seem so far away; I'm having trouble identifying steps to get to them."

## Maintenance

"I've taken some steps and they're working so far, what next?" "I'm clear about what my values and priorities are." "I've set myself a budget and have a better handle on my spending. Now what?" "I've got a lot of the information I need and got a plan, but I don't seem to be able to stick to it: How long do I have to give it to know if it's the right plan for me?" "I've worked hard on changing things and I don't want all that effort to go to waste."

## WHICH ONE FEELS MOST LIKE YOU?

In *contemplation*, you've got a feeling that you need to *do* something different, but you're not sure what. So you want to be clearer about what you're trying to achieve and the particular barriers you're trying to overcome. With *preparation*, you have ideas, but you can't currently get them into focus. What you need now is detail and a plan of action. With *action*, you have ideas and you've dipped your toe in the water by making small changes. Your actions now need to integrate your ideas so everything is related and working toward your goals. With *maintenance*, you're doing things that are working but aren't sure how to keep going forward. At this stage, motivating yourself to persist is important, as is building in a review so you can change your actions slightly as you develop new habits.

Now let's look at how you use that knowledge:

## WHERE YOU GO NEXT?

### Contemplation

You've already done some *consciousness raising*. In fact, that is what has brought you this far: You know you want to do something different around money in your life. You have become aware of how your values and motivations fit with the issues you face in your life (at this point, going to college, choosing a course of study, and, ultimately, moving into a career).

Another thing you can do is *ignite your emotions*, get passionate about your life. You can be pretty much anything you want to be in life if you really want to—let that excite and motivate you.

Remember your values, the things you really want. Not in an analytical sense, but what they mean to you deep down, what you want your life to be, what you'd tell a TV interviewer, what you'd look back on with real contentment in the future. That's what will drive you, so engage with that—however calm and analytical you are. Being calm and analytical are great tools; being passionate and really caring about what you're achieving are also great tools. Engage both in going forward.

If you care about doing something, like getting away from home to spread your wings and get some life experience at college, you've got a motivation to get over obstacles. That is fantastic. Of course, if you really care, really get passionate, you might be afraid that you are going to make mistakes or make wrong decisions about colleges, about where to put your money, what is worth buying, and what isn't. I can tell you for sure you will make wrong decisions sometimes; that's OK; that's what we all do; nobody in history has ever batted 1,000. That's why a lot of the suggestions in the book have included "experiment, try it on a small scale." Remember that if you're focused on your values and your goals, a wrong decision is a plus—you've gained useful information about what doesn't work for you, so you're another step nearer what does. Build in some review so you can learn from both success and mistakes (we talked about some meditation techniques earlier—take five minutes every once in a while to listen to yourself).

Another thing that you can do is *self-evaluation*. You've made a start on this with doing the exercises so far. You've looked at what you do with money and why, and possibly decided that you want to change your behavior. Remember, we have pathways in our heads that are easy to follow; that's what habits are. We develop those pathways and habits for a reason, the reason might not be a good one, as with a money story that isn't true, but they are still there and they can still be very well worn, powerful, and easy to follow. So it's common to try some new behaviors and then slip back to the old behavior because that seems easier for us.

So here's another exercise, to make that self-evaluation a bit more effective: Think of some behavior you want to change. For example, you might want to be less impulsive in your buying. At the moment, maybe you tend to have bought something before you even think about whether it's in your budget or whether it's a need or a want; as a result, you have a bunch of stuff you don't really use and no money for things that you'd use all the time!

Take a sheet of paper, and put a line down the middle. On the left side write "Changing," and on the right side write "Staying the Same." Now put a line across the middle, so you've divided the sheet into four boxes —and label them *pro* and *con* on each side. You've got a box for pros and one for cons of change, and one box for pros and one for cons of staying the same.

Now write into the appropriate boxes everything about being less impulsive (or whatever behavior you chose) that you can think of. Include as much as possible, in terms of your relationship to your friends, your image, your ambitions, the costs and benefits of change to others, everything. Don't edit yourself.

You need to get your motivations and your unconscious will out there in the open so you can see what is going on and get them lined up with your conscious intentions. This may be your first pass (see Table 10.1).

**Table 10.1**   Pros and Cons of Changing vs. Staying the Same, initial idea.

| Changing | Staying the Same |
|---|---|
| **Pro**<br>I'll feel more in control.<br>My family will respect me more.<br>I'll have the money to buy what I really want.<br>I'll have a better credit rating. | **Pro**<br>It's easier. |
| **Con**<br>It is hard to change habits. | **Con**<br>I won't be able to stick to my plans.<br>I might end up in debt.<br>I might have to go to my parents and beg for extra money.<br>It will be really embarrassing. |

Looks easy to change, right? You dive right in, ban yourself from shopping, make a list of your expenditures, decide you won't use your credit card, and so on. But now you start to notice another layer: You find you need your credit card when you shop "because it is convenient." You buy things that aren't in your budget "because they are on offer." Then you beat yourself up because you "can't change."

What it needs is a bit more thought and work. You need more time to think through what you are really getting out of whatever you do now and the habits you want to change—without judging yourself. So that table might, in reality, look more like this (see Table 10.2).

**Table 10.2**   Pros and Cons of Changing vs. Staying the Same, considered carefully.

| Changing | Staying the Same |
|---|---|
| **Pro**<br>I'll feel more in control.<br>My family will respect me more. | **Pro**<br>It's easier.<br>I'm comfortable the way I am. |

(*continued*)

**Table 10.2**   (Continued)

| Changing | Staying the Same |
| --- | --- |
| I'll have the money to buy what I really want. | I like the feeling of being able to buy stuff; I'd be a nerd if I always worried about every penny. |
| I'll have a better credit rating. | My friends think I'm cool. |
| **Con** | **Con** |
| It is hard to change habits. | I'll not be able to stick to my plans. |
| People will think I'm becoming a bore. | I might end up in debt. |
| Friends won't want to see me. | I might have to go to my parents and |
| Who will I actually be if I change? | beg for extra money. |
| What if I fail? | It will be really embarrassing. |

That's obviously more accurate!

If you do this exercise without either editing or judging yourself, you get a much better understanding of why you do what you currently do and what may keep you doing it. When you understand those things, it will be easier to make plans to change and to stick with the changes until they become your new habits.

Do that exercise, and get on with that self-evaluation, find out about you and it will make it easier for you to move from *contemplation* of changes to the next stage, *preparation*.

### Preparation

By "preparation," I mean the process of planning. And when you add planning to *commitment* and *passion*, you have a troika for success.

We talked about commitment in connection with one of the elements of setting useful goals: writing them down helps you commit. If your goal is "I'm going to get control of my finances, whatever it takes," your next step is the "how": breaking the goal into smaller steps, learning skills and techniques to do it. This is where planning comes in.

As part of the "how to," there are a number of skills and techniques that help. One is *environmental control*. Although it is only one of the areas you can work on, it is one of the most powerful and certainly the most commonly advised.

What you are doing is changing the environment you operate in—because you have realized that it may be contributing to keeping things as they are. There are three main ways that you can do that. You can:

Change features of the environment.

Change the cues in the environment.

Give yourself different cues.

One way to change the environment is *literally to change it.* If you find that you spend a lot of money that you don't mean to spend when you go into particular shops, a type of mall or visit a specific website, avoid those places for a while! Stay away from what you find really tempting for a set time, and work on being able to shop without giving in to temptation in a less pressured environment. The idea is to build up your confidence and distract your brain from its well-worn path by controlling the environment that you're in. The first time may be hard, the second time will be slightly easier, and over your "experiment timeframe" (say 30 days), you will retrain your brain away from the "stimulus/response" pattern it has been used to. If you try to use "willpower" and walk past loads of shops (or browse sites) that are really tempting, you're setting yourself up to fail.

That might sound like I'm saying you lack willpower. No, I'm saying everybody, you, me, all of us, has a human brain and it's wired so that some tactics work and some don't. Willpower alone doesn't work, but smart tactics work like a charm.

The reason we know this is that there's a classic experiment (try searching for "marshmallow experiment," seriously!). In this, children were offered a sweet and told that they could eat it now, but if they waited to eat the sweet, they would get a bag of sweets in 10 minutes. In theory, around a particular age, children learn to take less reward (or none) now, in order to have a bigger reward later.

The trouble is, that's theory! In reality, all of us find it easy to eat the sweet now; we all like to have it this minute, not to have to wait—everybody is like that, however old or young she or he is. So we tend to buy the "immediate want" (eat the sweet) now instead of waiting a while to get the "real need" (the bag of sweets) later.

The common factor in the analysis of children (and adults) who can manage to wait is that they "cover up" the sweet and got involved in doing something else. Those two tactics—covering up and getting involved in another activity—helped the children to avoid thinking about how nice the sweet would be, how much they want it, how hungry they are. By contrast, the children who didn't use those tactics kept looking at the sweet, thought about eating it, and tried simply to resist by "willpower." And the children in the first group, it turns out, were more successful in their careers and lives because of the tactics that served them in the marshmallow experiment.

That's why I say that willpower isn't the way to do it, because it really doesn't work with the way your brain is wired, and it doesn't work in practical terms. But if you "cover it up," don't walk past those stores for example, you're using the smart tactic of controlling the environment and increasing your likelihood of success.

You can change the environment by setting up your work area. If you habitually put bank statements, credit card and phone bills, and so on into a drawer to try to forget them, change that environment. Find a place to put them where you'll see them whenever you're doing something you do regularly, like put them on your computer so you have to move them every time.

If you put the papers away and you ignore them when they're away, then even if you put them away neatly in a file drawer, you'll ignore them. You might not mean to, but you will. It's about changing habits. Think of the sweet experiment. If the papers are away, they're covered up—therefore you can ignore them. If they are there, in front of you, you keep thinking about them, you can't ignore them, you keep seeing them, and they irritate you. In the end, you have to do something with them. It might be to chuck them in the drawer, but you can't ignore them. If they're out of sight, you can, irrespective of good intentions, diary notes, and the like, forget about them. You have to change the environment in order to change the behavior. If they're not "out of sight," you have to keep thinking about them and eventually you'll deal with them out of sheer boredom!

From there, it's another small step to keeping track of where your money goes, and whether it fits into your plans. A good goal has small steps, remember.

Another way to change your environment is to change your social environment, your companions. If you've got a buddy that you tend to spend more with, you encourage one another with "dares" or compete to have the best, latest, or most hi-tech and fashionable, you might need to limit the exposure to that buddy or suggest different activities. This is often the hardest change to make. But you want to give yourself the best chance of success, so you want to surround yourself with friends who share and want the same type of success! It can feel like you're turning your back on your friends and stopping yourself from having any fun. Some clients think that's too hard; they decide that they will stop spending on what they don't really need, then go shopping with "the usual suspects," and end up right back in the same behavior. Changing the habit of amount of contact is easier—this is about learning to manage your patterns, not change someone else's! That's the point of environmental control; if you prepare the environment (social and physical) in advance, you give yourself the best chance to help yourself change.

Another cue you can give yourself relies on the child in us all. You like silliness—even if you're seen (or want to be seen) as very mature and serious! I used to be amazed that charity fund raisers would have big images of things (the church steeple, a space rocket, a big thermometer) and color it in as they raised money. It seemed so childish to me (a "mature" 14 year old!), and I realized as I got older and studied psychology that they do it because it works—pictures, images, visual gags engage us and we want to fill the image up. Pictures of role models, those that inspire you, sayings that sum up what you want to achieve in life, drawings of the life you want—they might seem like putting up pictures of the rock star you had a crush on, but they're actually very powerful. They keep giving you cues about what you're trying to do. You can put them where you'll see them regularly, like on your bathroom mirror.

Or you can give yourself another type of cue. Imagine that you have an outline image of the vacation you're saving for, that you fill in as you accumulate the money. And you put a red dot (one of those little sticky circles you can get from a stationery store) on the image. And you have a red dot on your phone, your watch, your credit card. Every time you look at one of those things, which will be many times a day, you'll be reminded of what you're saving for.

You can build in variations of those to suit yourself. Allow yourself some silliness and creativity that work for you. You want things that give you the cue to remember what you're trying to change for (your values and goals), that encourage you to perform useful behaviors that you're working on, and that discourage you from returning to the old behaviors that you want to change.

You can also change your own cues. You can set up reminders on your phone or other organizer, to help you think of and do the new habits. For example, you can set reminders about checking your bank statement and settling the bills a couple of days before the end of the month—instead of realizing you haven't paid them a few days too late! You can set reminders to interrupt automatic behavior: Imagine that you are trying to keep track of where your cash goes and want to make a note of what you spend but you keep forgetting to jot it down. Put your cash in a wallet and put an elastic band round the opener—you can't take out cash without removing the band, so you can't just hand out money and forget to note it down, you have to remove the band and that gives you the cue to make a note.

Another way to change things is to change the action you take to your own cues. If you feel depressed or bored and that automatically lights up the bit of your brain that tells you "retail therapy is the answer, who cares about the question," find a new habit as a "go to" behavior (and keep reminding yourself about it until it becomes a habit). One of the best is to work out, run or generally do something active. Other similar ideas are progressive relaxation, meditation, yoga, and Tai Chi, but it can be anything else that's useful. You can tackle the project you keep putting off, phone a friend, do something other than whatever behavior you want to avoid.

I mentioned exercise and meditative practices particularly for a reason, because they are some of the best alternatives to substitute for any habit you are trying to change. You get fitter and healthier (mentally and/or physically), and it takes your mind off the ineffective habit.

To achieve your goals, you need to change the habits that are hurting you and make them ones that help you. If you start to break the links between the current trigger and your old response, give yourself cues for different behavior, or make the trigger a cue for the new, and positive, response, you start to change your habits. And, you may see this behavior spill into other areas of your life.

### Action

Environmental control is helpful in this stage, as are some others, such as *countering* and *helping relationships*.

Countering is about dealing with thoughts that don't help you. Part of that can be provided by things like exercise, meditation, mindfulness, and other alternatives to whatever habit you are trying to break. We've looked at mindfulness in relation to stress reduction and making better decisions, and it can be really helpful when you get into those situations where you start to doubt yourself, wonder whether what you're doing is going to work, consider just giving up because you can't do it. You can, and you know you can really; it's just your mind (like everybody's) is largely unconscious, and it tends to run on its own much of the time—so it doesn't always give you messages that fit with "the new you." It gives you messages based on the pathways, your money story, as it used to be. When there's a conflict (as there's bound to be when you're trying to change habits), sometimes you get those messages that try to get you to stay where you were instead of go where you want, because that's what your subconscious mind is used to and feels safer with. Eventually, as your new habits take root, things will settle down and your subconscious will be happy and want to stay with the "new you!" Until that happens, you will get times when it seems you can't do anything right and all your work is for nothing, and mindfulness, as well as physical exercise and working on your new habits, will help you counter those feelings.

You can also work on specific feelings directly, using the ABC technique that I talked about in Chapter 2. The idea is to give you some arguments to use on your subconscious, so when those negative thoughts arise, you can dispute them, you can argue for the new you, for the habits you want to develop to be the person you want to be.

I mentioned helping relationships earlier on. In the planning stage, it can be useful to enlist trustworthy friends. Friends are great for building commitment because if you tell them what you're doing, you've got that added incentive to stick with it. If you keep your attempts to change your behavior to yourself, you can quietly go back to your old habits with nobody any the wiser. You'll remember that in terms of goals in Chapter 3, where the written goals seem to help because they are a commitment that you are known to have made.

Enlisting friends can be a blessing or a curse, mind you. What you want is the friend who will ask you how much you really want something on a scale of one to ten, and tell you to wait until your desire is at least at a "nine" level before you have it! You want to enlist helpers who will be kind and encouraging, but firm. And you want friends who will call you out if you are depending on them to change your habit: This is a collaboration, not a nanny state, and it is you who want to change. So you have to take the responsibility and not blame your friends if you don't change.

Like Mark and his father, whom we talked about in Chapters 2 and 3, we sometimes need "tough love"; people who will help us not by letting us be the way we are now, but by giving us the opportunity to change. So if you're looking for a friend to help you, make sure you pick the ones that will help with what you want to do and become, not ones who will help to keep you where you are now. And make sure they know what you're trying to do, so that they can help you stay on track. Ideally they'll kid with you but also build you up.

## Maintenance

You may want some more environmental control, employ countering, enlist helping relationships, or renew your commitment.

One thing that can help with commitment is *rewarding* yourself. Not a reward that involves spending much (if any) money, obviously! What you are trying to do is reinforce your new behaviors. Even if it seems trivial, a mental "pat on the back," an encouraging message to yourself in your diary or planner, taking a few moments to think how well you've done today, all helps. It makes you feel more in control and builds your self-belief. It also encourages you to "keep up the good work."

As with the "red dot" idea, you can remind yourself of your goals (think of the shape of the plane that's taking you on your "graduation trip," that's filling in as you approach your savings target), of affirmations and encouraging messages ("That's two months of knowing what I'm spending, working on my goals, checking on my bills—I've got this nailed").

You can also, with the right helping relationships, get some similar reward from friends; they can congratulate you and give you feedback that helps your resolve. In general, positive reinforcement (rewards, praise, and so on for getting it right) is more effective in helping people to learn a new behavior than negative reinforcement (beating yourself up or being criticized when you get it wrong).

On an ongoing basis, you will also probably want to do some self-evaluation. Your current situation changes, and as you move through change, your objectives (such as which shops to avoid or particular habits to change) may shift, your relationships with people may alter, the rewards that are appropriate may change, and your goals might become different.

## STICKING WITH IT

When you've decided on your values, set your goals, and planned your actions, you can start to change your behaviors so that you can work on the plan. You might need to be organized in a different way or to change your money story; there are many different actions that you might want to change to reach your unique goals and values. We've looked at some of the key points so if you look through those stages of change, pick the changes you want to make, and use your knowledge of yourself, you'll be able to find changes that you can make that will help you be the way you want to be, to achieve the life you want.

But when you decide on changes in behaviors or habits, you also have to stick with those changes until they become "the way I am" and you don't have to work at them any more.

There are, literally, thousands of things you might do to help yourself change and I only have room for a few. But here are some principles, and if you think about them and apply them to your own new behaviors, they will help you stick with them.

## Use Your Bank Account

Whether you are saving to invest, to pay regular bills, for a special event, whatever, set things up so it's done automatically—preferably just after money goes into your account. Three reasons for that:

1. It takes the effort out of it. You don't have to remember or change your behavior; you just set things up.
2. It uses your human laziness and inertia. If you think "one day I'll get organized," it means you're not and you identify yourself as disorganized. If you sort it out and think "I'm sorted, my bills are paid, my savings are building," hey, you're in control of your finance; that's just the way you are.
3. It puts the money out of your reach. If you have it saved, committed, used first up, I'm certain you can spend what is left! If you think "if I have some money at the end of the month, I'll save it," you won't; everybody can spend the remainder that isn't saved; nobody can save the remainder of what isn't spent, because it all gets spent!

## If You Want to "Ring Fence" Money, Make It Special

Imagine that you have an aged ancestor (great grandfather, say) that you've always loved and who leaves you $50,000. On his deathbed, he whispers to you that he left you the money because you were always his favorite and he hopes you'll use it for your college fund. Tell me, could you splash that money on music downloads, a party or two, some clothes? Or would you feel that you'd really have to use it for college, as a down payment on an apartment, or something really permanent, a sort of memorial?

Most people in finance will tell you that you *shouldn't* feel like that, that money is just money and it's all the same. Maybe that's so in theory, but this is your world, and that gift has meaning for you. You do feel like money is different depending on where it came from (it's what I mentioned are called mental accounts) and given that situation you'd probably rather sell a kidney than waste that money on something trivial.

If you want to keep money safe and ensure it isn't spent, you don't have to lock it away in Fort Knox (although having extra safeguards doesn't hurt). You just create for yourself a "special" fund that, in your mind, is totally untouchable: It's the "great grandpa's memorial savings fund" or something. And the fantastic thing is that if you are very susceptible to spending wildly on credit cards and generally have a tendency to powerful "mental accounting," your "special" money will be extra special; your mind will set up a block on wasting it that is really strong.

## Decide What Is Special and Treat All Other Money as Earned Money

We all have mental accounts to some extent and treat some money (credit cards, tax rebates, lottery wins, and so on) as "play money" and some money as "real" money.

So treat everything that isn't special as "earned money." Think about it as if you had to work long hours on a Saturday night in some horrible job to earn it. Fix in your mind that your money—wherever it came from, on credit, as a gift, that you found in the street—is money you had to sweat and suffer for. To bolster your mental vision of the money, you can stick a "post-it" note to your credit card to tell you to think "would I buy it, and how much would I pay, if I had to pay from my earned money?"

## Separate Usable and Necessary Money

Some money will be usable. That means you can use it to pay day-to-day expenses and so on. You may also have a special fund for your long-term goals.

And you can set up a "necessary funds" account for the regular bills (the "needs")—rent, tuition, food, and so on. You put into it enough money to cover those amounts. Then the big bills and regular expenses, the holiday fund, hair styling, or whatever are your "necessary" expenses are taken care of. If you set up your special and necessary funds and think of them as being important, you will be surprised how reluctant you are to dip into them for trivial things. You accumulate money a lot faster for your goals and have the money for necessary expenses when you need it.

Also, if you work on your mental accounting and use that necessary account only to pay bills that it is designated to cover, you will not tend to spend money if you get a while without big bills and can build a cushion for surprises (the bike is stolen or the tire on the car goes flat).

The money will accumulate in the necessary fund and the usable money will be all you spend. This becomes your new habit, the way you are, and it will become a conscious effort to go back to habits that didn't work for you. And now you have a very simple checklist for spending. If you consider buying something, just ask yourself these two questions:

- Is it a long-term goal so it comes from "special" money?
- Is it covered by what you put into the necessary fund?
- If neither of those applies, then whether it is for an emergency, is something you think you really need, or just fancy having, it ought to come from your usable money.

- If you can't afford it from usable money, then you can't afford it. For example, if you don't contribute to the special fund to cover your holiday, then the holiday has to come out of your usable money or you can't afford it. If the fund won't cover your credit card, you can't use the card.

### Set Up a "Tithe" of Any Windfall

This can be tithing in the traditional sense (paying a sum, usually a tenth, of your money to a charity, typically your church). It is a good way to increase happiness.

You can also "tithe" to yourself. Rather than get a tax rebate, bonus, gift, overtime payment, or whatever and have it burn a hole in your pocket, put some amount, maybe all of it (but see the idea about treating yourself, later on), into your savings, your "special fund" or "necessary" account.

You can apply this to anything, pay rises, unexpected gratuities—if you commit to putting a proportion of that money away, it has several effects. It makes you feel good, it identifies you to yourself as a saver, and it puts the saving away as soon as possible (just because "start early" is simplistic, doesn't mean it's not a good idea!).

### Have a Reward Account

If you are trying to train yourself to act differently, it can help to reward yourself (remember the point in "maintenance" earlier). You can tithe from windfalls or put a regular amount away as "fun money" as mentioned in the last chapter. This reinforces your new behaviors. So, *if* you're sticking with your plans, you might treat yourself to something special that doesn't cost more than you've got in the "fun" account. If what you want is a bit more than you've got, you can set it as a short-term goal: put away a bit of money each month and treat yourself. You can get a great sense of accomplishment from being proactive and saving for something—along with feeling the virtuous glow of having done it, you are proving to yourself that it is possible to develop new habits that work for you, not against you.

### Protect Your Assets

Sometimes you may need insurance on things of value, like computers. Other times you find out the premiums are more than you'd be able to claim, or you know you'll have to replace something when it goes out of date (again, like computers every few years) and insurance won't cover "wear and tear." If you've got things that you might need to replace, you can check out the replacement cost and the estimated life, work out what it adds up to monthly, and put that amount away each month. So if it's $600 and you figure it will last for 4 years, that's about $12–13 a month. Put that away, and when you need to replace it—there you go, you've got the money ready.

### Brainstorm Your Options

I've tried to suggest things to think about, but I don't have room to suggest more than a fraction of what I know that might work for you—and I don't know you nearly as well as you do!

So when you're looking at actions, don't restrict yourself, think crazy, really go for it, and don't censor the ideas. When you've got as many as you can, do a work out, sleep on it, give yourself a break, and come back to it and brainstorm it again—I guarantee you'll come up with more. When you've really come up with every idea, you can still talk to friends, family, and advisors to gather ideas you hadn't considered—see if they trigger anything for you. Only after you've got masses of ideas do you want to narrow down to the practical—it's proven over and over again, get the ideas first and then critique them; it works way better. You may have time limits on gathering information—remember, use your goals as a filter to keep you headed in the direction you want.

You can apply this not just to ideas for change, to control the environment, manage cues, and so on; you can expand your horizons by brainstorming on ways to generate more money if you find you need it. To start you off: Are there things you can sell that you don't need? Have you got a hobby or interest that could produce earnings: website designing, cake making, gardening? There are books on options for home businesses and other extra sources of income; try the library; it can trigger your creativity.

### Make the Best Decisions You Can

That honestly isn't like the advice to the pitcher "throw strikes!" It's about doing the best you can in the place where you are, not the best possible in all the world if things were different. None of us can get it right all the time because we can't foretell the future; we can all just do our best.

So don't be scared of making decisions; do the best you can—if it works, you learn something, and if it doesn't work, you learn something—it's a win-win!

Whether it's about what college to go to, the food plan to follow, what behaviors to change, what actions to take to change—whatever it is, you can do your best with decisions and generally the way to do your best is to be reasonably balanced between your emotions, reasoning, and intuitive senses.

We all get enthusiastic or depressed, feel we're right or we're stupid, that others are right or are idiots. We see things in absolutes. That's why things like mindfulness are useful. They help to give us balance.

Here are some other ways to get that balance and help you make the best decisions that you can.

Relate decisions to your values. If something makes you uneasy, think about why that is. If it's scary because it's new to you, maybe that's just an emotional reaction and it's worth considering even if you're afraid. If it seems to conflict with something that you really believe is important, even if it seems a good idea and it's likely to make you money, would you be comfortable with something that you thought was unethical?

Look at conflicting ideas. Actively seek out those who have opposite opinions to the ones you hold. If you're buying things, rival sales people can be handy—they'll give you different views of the same issue. Obviously, they'll be biased, but they give you more ideas than if you just look at things one way. And if you're thinking in one way about a problem, somebody who sees the world in a different way can sometimes give you really helpful ideas or give you equally useful confirmation that your initial decision was right for you.

Try to keep the people you use as advisors independent. If you ask a group, they will come to a consensus and merge to give you a "what everybody knows" view. If you ask them separately, you'll get some mainstream views, some really wild and wacky ones, and some well to either side of the mainstream. That gives you loads of options; all of which may be things you've never thought of. You might reject them all in the end and go with what you first thought, but if that happens, you can have a lot of confidence that yours was the best decision you could have made. And you may get some great options that you would never have thought of.

Check on others' reasoning. Ask them not just what they'd do but what they'd look at, how they would weigh up the options, the pros and cons. What do you think are the key things to consider and why? It gives you different ways to think and makes you notice different features of the environment (remember the "pros and cons" from earlier).

Avoid making the decision during periods of anxiety or enthusiasm; you'll likely either panic or get overconfident. Mindfulness is a useful way to get some distance from your emotions. You can also imagine you're a consultant or that a friend came to you with the same problem: What advice would you give? As with the ABC idea in Chapter 2, it takes some of the emotional heat out of the situation, and you're more likely to make the best decision you can.

There are situations where you've thought about something and you really don't know which choice you prefer. I've known people really agonize over this, but there is a simple way to find out what you want (remember, sometimes that is unconscious, and it's hard to decide what is really important to you). It sounds strange, but toss a coin or cut a pack of cards (decide beforehand which outcome means which choice). You don't have to go with that, but if you're really not bothered, it will save time! The real value is that what it usually does is to open up your subconscious to you. When I've done it myself (and I have, quite often), I've always had a hope that a particular result would come up while the coin was in the air. I hadn't know that, but suddenly I knew something about what I wanted that I hadn't known before. Sometimes that made my choice for me, sometimes it prompted me to reexamine my options and do something different altogether, but if I've genuinely not known what I wanted or which choice to make, it's always been useful.

### SUMMARY

Check what "stage" you're at, to give you an idea of what actions are likely to be helpful.

Depending on the stage you're at, look at the types of actions that are likely to be most useful to you at this point.

Plan some little actions you can take and experiment with, to see how they work and how your attitudes shift. Then plan some more!

Review your progress on your actions and your plans, and check periodically where you are in terms of "stage"—you may have moved on, so you may need to consider some new actions to keep things moving the way you want.

Repeat the development and implementation of little actions, experiments, to keep heading toward your goals.

Remember, you can change your habits and your money story. It's about using effective tactics, not being superhuman and having infinite willpower.

And remember that you are the most important thing—your money is simply a tool to get you the happy life that you want. You can get that life; you can achieve your values—it may take some work, but there's no doubt at all that you can do it.

# Afterword

You've now got the tools to learn more about how you think and what you want from life. And you've got a lot of ideas for questions to ask to find out what you want to know and ways to think about what you want to do with the answers.

I thought about suggesting lots of websites (apart from the ones mentioned in the book), suggesting more books to read (apart from the ones mentioned), and so on. In the end, I decided against it, because the idea is to get you to focus on what **you** want and will find useful, not what *I* think you *might* want or find useful!

But there's one thing that I've realized might be helpful. Personally I don't like it when well-meaning people try to give me help I don't want. But that's me and many people like guidelines; they can feel a bit lost without them. And a guideline I often get asked for is the proportion of money that might go into different areas. So here's that sort of guideline.

Remember, it is a guideline. It's not what you *ought* to spend or anything else; it's just to give you a starting point.

Housing: 25–30 percent
Transport: 10–15 percent
Utilities: 5–10 percent (including cellular phone)
Food: 10–20 percent (including eating out)
Personal Items: 15 percent (including clothing, entertainment, vacation)

Savings: 10 percent
Donations: 5–10 percent

If you are trying to get started, having some idea of what is *typical* might be a help to you. Try this out, see what's different, and adjust for your priorities (e.g., if you ride a bike, the "transport" line may be five percent. But don't forget holiday trips home!). Of course, once you get your own budget sorted out and you work with it for a while, you can use that for a guideline in future: What you've spent and the proportions you've spent it on during your first year are a far better guide for your second and subsequent years than anything that I can suggest. And if the word "budget" makes you feel like you are wearing a straitjacket, then call it your "adventure plan" or your "roadmap!"

With one proviso—whatever you do, you want the proportions to add up to 100 percent or less! If it is less, then you've got some more money to allocate where you want (savings? an adventure fund?), which is great. Just make sure you haven't missed anything (go through the lists) and congratulate yourself. If you are over 100 percent, however, you definitely need to go over your figures again and really look at trade-offs you can make to get to 100 percent and to where you want to go!

I hope you've enjoyed this guide and look forward to answering any additional questions you might have. So feel free to e-mail either me (kim@stephenson-consulting.co.uk) or my coauthor, Ann Hutchins (ann@abhutchins.com), and we'll get back to you. Good luck, have fun, and get your money working for you, instead of you working for your money!

# Index

happiness, 11, 17–18, 19 n.4, 134;
wasteful, 26, 59, 69, 80, 82–85, 94,
94 nn.1–3, 100, 104–5, 107, 159
Stages of change, 152–63. *See also*
Action; Contemplation;
Maintenance; Preparation
Stocks. *See* shares
Strengths, 5, 12–13, 18, 36, 151.
*See also* Values
Stress: biology of, 22, 41, 67;
control, 14–15, 19 n.5, 31–32, 39,
41, 158, 160–61; impact on
decision making, 14–15, 17, 21,
32, 161, 168; impact on mental
health, 19 n.5, 21, 31,
147, 152, 168

Teasdale, John, 19 n.5
Thinking: conscious, 22, 29, 32–33,
46, 94, 156; helpful, 1–3, 8–9,
11–13, 17, 22, 24, 26, 28–33, 49,
53–55, 60–61, 71, 75, 78, 89–90,
92, 94, 101, 103–7, 109, 123–24,
126, 129, 132, 141, 144, 153,
155–65, 167–68; intuitive/
unconscious, 22–24, 26, 29–30,
33, 41–42, 46, 79, 81–87, 168–69;
logical/rational, 22, 24, 87;
unhelpful, 15, 36, 38, 65, 68, 95,
104, 118, 134, 161–62; watching
thoughts, 16–17. *See also* Decision
making

Time: in investment, 112, 115–21,
123–25, 128, 132, 145–46, 148.
*See also* Investment
Transtheoretical model
of change, 152
Travel: around campus, 61, 76, 111,
141; to college, 77, 141; vacation,
137, 141

Vacation job, 3–5, 44–45, 47, 117,
144, 146
Values: determining, 10–13, 49, 54,
163; and goals, 37–39, 41–42, 49,
51, 54, 102, 131–32, 134–36,
152–53, 155, 163; and happiness,
5–6, 8, 13, 18, 22–23, 27, 37–39,
41–42, 59, 66, 75, 77, 89, 96, 145,
154, 160, 168–69; monetary, 10,
63, 85, 87, 91, 94, 97, 112–13,
121, 125, 128–29, 146, 166

Wants. *See* Needs v wants
Websites: college and store,
58, 93, 158; useful resource, 13,
16, 18 n.1, 19 nn.4–5, 61,
71, 74, 93
Williams, Mark, 19 n.5
Willpower, 152, 158, 169
Wilson, Stephanie, 94 n.2
Windfall money, 9

Zhang, Maggie, 94 n.3

**About the Authors**

KIM STEPHENSON, CPSYCHOL, ACII, Dip PFS, is the director of Stephenson Consulting. His published work includes *Taming the Pound: Making Money Your Servant, Not Your Master,* a book on the practical use of psychology in financial planning nominated for a British Psychological Society prize for best popular science book of the year. He is qualified and has practiced professionally as both a financial adviser and an industrial and organizational psychologist.

ANN B. HUTCHINS, CFC, ACC, is the principal of Ann B. Hutchins Financial Coach. She received her MBA in finance from Babson College in Wellesley, MA, and BA in American Studies from Hamilton College in Clinton, NY.